Date Due

Dec 17'69			
	PRINTED	IN U. S. A.	

BIG FISH, LITTLE FISH

Big Fish, Little Fish

A new
comedy
by
**Hugh
Wheeler**

Random House
New York

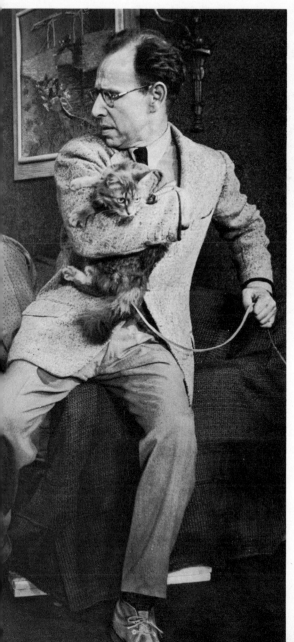

For
ELIZABETH BEERBOHM,
with love

BIG FISH, LITTLE FISH *was first presented by Lewis Allen and Ben Edwards, in association with Joseph I. Levine, at the ANTA Theatre, New York City, on March 15, 1961, with the following cast:*

(IN ORDER OF APPEARANCE)

EDITH MAITLAND	Ruth White
JIMMIE LUTON	Hume Cronyn
WILLIAM BAKER	Jason Robards, Jr.
BASIL SMYTHE	Martin Gabel
HILDA ROSE	Elizabeth Wilson
RONNIE JOHNSON	George Grizzard
PAUL STUMPFIG	George Voskovec

Directed by John Gielgud

Setting and lighting by Ben Edwards

Costumes by Mary Grant

(Mr. Allen producing for Allen-Hodgdon Productions)

The play is set in William Baker's New York apartment in the East Thirties.

The time is the present.

ACT ONE

SCENE 1: Early evening of a March day.

SCENE 2: Late that night.

ACT TWO

SCENE 1: 8:30 the next morning.

SCENE 2: Two weeks later. Saturday morning, 11:30 A.M.

ACT THREE

SCENE 1: That evening at 6:55 P.M.

SCENE 2: One week later.

ACT ONE

Scene One

The living room of WILLIAM BAKER's *two-room bachelor apartment in the East Thirties of Manhattan. It is comfortable enough, with no sense of style; bargains from Macy's are mingled with a few undistinguished Victorian heirlooms from* WILLIAM's *mother's home in Portland, Oregon. The general effect is saved from drabness by a certain air of coziness.*

Right of the rear wall is a small hallway with closet leading to the front door, beyond which are visible a landing and the last few stairs coming up from the lower floors. Center left, in this order, are a bathroom (whose interior is visible when the door is open) and a kitchenette half concealed behind a screen. Left rear is a door to the bedroom, downstage from which is a couch which can serve as an extra bed. Right front a drop-leaf table is set up for a party of six.

At rise, EDITH MAITLAND *is taking an old lampshade off a standard lamp and replacing it with a new one which is gaudily hand painted, with scarlet-coated huntsmen in full flight. The paper which has wrapped it is on the floor. Her coat and hat are on the couch.* EDITH MAITLAND *is an ordinary, wellish-to-do New Jersey wife, mother and grandmother, fiftyish, unrecognizable from the other matrons of her suburban community.*

As she fiddles with the shades, JIMMIE LUTON *hurries up the stairs in a coat, with an overnight bag. He tries to let himself in the front door with a key but is stopped by the chain which is in place.* JIMMIE LUTON, *thin, fifty, with glasses, is excitable and affectionate. Although he is ceaselessly scolding, he worships* WILLIAM BAKER, *the owner of the apartment, who is, in fact, his whole life.*

JIMMIE (*Off*) Chain, chain, goddam chain. William, William . . .

EDITH It's all right, Jimmie. I'm coming.
    (*She takes the chain off*)

JIMMIE (*Entering*) You've been here for hours, I suppose. I had classes until four. My God, the weather and all those stairs.

EDITH I took an early bus from Tomsville.

JIMMIE And you're spending the night, I suppose.

EDITH Of course.

JIMMIE Isn't William back yet?

EDITH Not yet. I guess he's working late.

JIMMIE The bastards. At least they could have let him off early on his birthday. You'll be delighted to hear your bloody bridge party has stuck me with William's Philharmonic ticket. I asked all the wretched little girls in my art class, but no one would go. My God, isn't music art?

EDITH I don't see why you bother to go yourself. Why don't you just stay and cut in?

JIMMIE Bridge? On Philharmonic night? As if culture was a punishment or something? I hope I'm not as intellectually dead as all that—even to honor and worship at William's

4

birthday shrine. (*Sees the new "gift" lampshade*) For the love of God, where did that come from?

EDITH It's my birthday present for William.

JIMMIE And you thinking you're so artistic, lunching at the Museum of Modern Art. How's that dinner you came to cook? Chaos as usual, I suppose.

EDITH Everything's done. The table and everything. Look, Jimmie, after I came in from Tomsville, I trudged over to Dennison's and got some party favors. Poppers and streamers too.

JIMMIE Poppers, streamers. Bourgeois. Suburban.
(WILLIAM *lets himself in. He is wearing a coat and carrying the* Saturday Review. WILLIAM BAKER, *in his late forties, is the center and "king" of the little group. He is a bachelor who has a minor executive position in a textbook publishing house. His most characteristic feature is his great kindness and sweetness. Calm, soft-spoken and infinitely patient with the constant emotional demands made upon him by his little circle of admirers, he is quietly amused at everyone, including himself. Like most people who attract the lonely and the misfits, he has his own tensions and insecurities although they scarcely ever show. We do not know how much he depends on the adoration which is lavished upon him by his flock*)

WILLIAM Hey, hey.
(EDITH *runs toward him.* JIMMIE, *somewhat diffident, hovers*)

EDITH Happy birthday, William.

5

WILLIAM (*Kissing her*)   Well, here you are—with your shining evening face. Sorry I'm late. Everything under control?

EDITH   My, you look fine tonight.

WILLIAM   Well, that's a comfort.

JIMMIE (*As* WILLIAM *comes to him*)   Happy birthday, William.

WILLIAM   Thank you, Jimmie. How are those art students of yours?

JIMMIE   Moronic, as usual.

WILLIAM   Did Viola call?

EDITH   The Lady from Philadelphia? Why, no, William. She hasn't called.

JIMMIE   That'd be all we need, the Lady from Philadelphia calling up all evening making that goddam dog bark Happy Birthday to you over the phone.

EDITH   Poor old thing. (*As* WILLIAM *sits she stands coquettishly behind him, cupping her hands over his eyes*)   William, William—look, my present.
    (*She releases him*)

WILLIAM (*Looking happily at the lampshade*)   *It's terribly* handsome. All those horses. See how they gallop.
    (*During this exchange,* JIMMIE *has sneaked a package out of his overnight bag and put it on the sideboard*)

EDITH   I went to the top salesman at B. Altman's and asked what was the very smartest lampshade for a conservative bachelor. He said everyone's reverting to Tavern British. But if you don't like it, I can always take it back and get a credit.

JIMMIE   Get the credit. (*He is surveying the set table*) Oh, William, you're not going to use those dreadful old blue place mats. Why don't you use the ones I brought you from Greece?

WILLIAM   It's a gesture to Basil. He gave them to me on my birthday five years ago.

JIMMIE   I gave you the ones from Greece, didn't I? Why not make a gesture to me?

EDITH   Basil's so sensitive.

JIMMIE   So just because Basil's sensitive you're making a gesture to him?

WILLIAM   That's right.

JIMMIE   There's only one gesture I'd make to Basil.
(*He makes it. By now he has unwrapped his package to reveal two large chunky red candles, which he replaces for the ones already being used on the dinner table*)

EDITH   Oh, where did those terrible red candles come from?

JIMMIE   They're my birthday present to William. They're Portuguese. Portuguese altar candles. And if *you* don't like them that's just too bad.

WILLIAM   Portuguese altar candles. No one but you could have thought of that, Jimmie. They couldn't be more festive. Thank you. Ronnie's coming. He called about an hour ago from Grand Central.

EDITH   For dinner?

JIMMIE   Well, well, aren't you the privileged one.

EDITH He won't be spending the night, will he?

WILLIAM He usually does. Jimmie can bring out the cot.

EDITH Is Jimmie staying too?

JIMMIE What do you expect me to do? Sleep on the sidewalk like some Bowery bum? (*Indicating the couch*) That sofa is mine.

EDITH I hadn't planned for all this.

WILLIAM Then it makes a pleasant surprise, doesn't it?

EDITH (*Counting on fingers*) With Ronnie for dinner that makes six of us. Oh, well, I guess I can stretch the mock hollandaise somehow.
  (*She goes into the kitchenette*)

JIMMIE Fancy Ronnie remembering your birthday.

WILLIAM He sometimes does.

JIMMIE Bet he didn't come down specially for it. Bet he had something else to do.

WILLIAM As a matter of fact, some Swiss publishing friend of his is here looking for a translator or something and Ronnie said he'd help.

JIMMIE Help—what? Find a translator?

WILLIAM That's what I gathered.

JIMMIE And you didn't say anything?

WILLIAM What should I have said?

JIMMIE My God, you—you with your French, your Spanish, your German. Why not you?

WILLIAM It's obviously an important job. They'll need someone very imposing.

JIMMIE And you're not someone imposing? My God, when that old bastard fired you from Merton, you could have done anything. (*There is a rather awkward pause at this and* WILLIAM *goes into the bathroom, leaving the door ajar.* JIMMIE *continues, railing*) If you'd had any push, you could have been President of the United States or Doubleday. Twenty years buried in the same dreary department. A sub, sub editor . . .

WILLIAM (*From the bathroom*) Nineteen years and a bit.

JIMMIE Doing all the work, wallowing in obscurity. Okay, so you're not going to talk to Ronnie?

WILLIAM I wouldn't dream of it. If he'd thought of me, he'd have mentioned it.
(*He comes out of the bathroom*)

EDITH (*Entering from the kitchenette*) What's Jimmie beefing about now?

WILLIAM Nothing. He's just trying to further my career. You know how he always likes to boost me.

EDITH As if you needed boosting.
(*She hands him a festive red party shirt which has been hanging on the kitchen screen, and exits to the bedroom*)

JIMMIE You and your women. My God, you'd sleep with anyone who asked you, wouldn't you? Anyone. Whistler's mother.

WILLIAM (*Putting on his shirt*) She doesn't want to do it much any more. Not Whistler's mother. Edith.

JIMMIE I bet.

WILLIAM She doesn't. It's true. Not often.

JIMMIE Then why does she always come crashing up here the moment that terrible husband of hers goes away? What's she been committing for the last twenty-five years? Denatured adultery?

WILLIAM It isn't twenty-five years. If you want to be accurate, it's . . .

JIMMIE Nineteen years and a bit. And she doesn't want to do it any more?

WILLIAM Not often.

JIMMIE God, what a wonderful romance. What does she come for then if she doesn't want to do it?

WILLIAM Because she's used to me, I guess.

JIMMIE Isn't she used to her husband?

WILLIAM Probably.

JIMMIE And isn't she used to her goddam daughters and sons-in-law and grandchildren?

WILLIAM Probably.

JIMMIE Then why does she need being used to you, too?

WILLIAM You need everything you can get.

JIMMIE But she's a bore.

WILLIAM I'm a bore. You're a bore.

JIMMIE Maybe I am, but I try not to be. I try to keep up with things, get new ideas.

WILLIAM I'm very fond of her.
(EDITH *comes out of the bedroom*)

WILLIAM Well, Jimmie, aren't you going to be barman and fix Edith a drink?

JIMMIE What do you want, Edith? A martini?

EDITH That suits me fine. But I'll do it. I was just going to fix one for William, anyway.

JIMMIE You don't have to, thank you very much. That happens to be my job.
(*He exits to the kitchen. The sound of a church chime is heard*)

EDITH My, isn't that a new noise?

WILLIAM Some guy bequeathed chimes to the church.

EDITH Darling, do you realize it's almost twenty years since the *S.S. Pastores?* Twenty years less a month. April twenty-sixth, it was.

WILLIAM At ten thirty-five. The Bouillon Hour.

EDITH We could think of tonight as a celebration for that too, couldn't we? Your birthday and our first meeting. Strange, the very first moment I saw you in that deck chair, I knew.

WILLIAM Feminine intuition.

EDITH   Yes, that's what it was. And I knew there was something that was making you unhappy too. Of course I had no idea about Merton and all that drama. But I knew there was something. I could help him, I thought. Then Kenneth came up in that yachting cap, remember?

WILLIAM   And carried you off to victory in the Married Couples Shuffleboard Contest. Is that husband of yours still a demon at shuffleboard?

EDITH   Oh, yes, he still has a knack for things like that. Odd, isn't it? I used to feel so guilty about Kenneth in those days. And now it seems so natural. My, we've been lucky in life, haven't we?

WILLIAM   It's a bitch of a doublecrostic this week.

EDITH   I don't know how you work those things. I just don't know.
   (JIMMIE *returns with drinks*)

JIMMIE   Here, Edith, taste this. See if it's cold enough for you.

EDITH   Delicious.

JIMMIE   Well, it'll have to do.
   (*He gives* WILLIAM *a drink*)

EDITH   There, William. Just what you need after that long day at the office.
   (BASIL *and* HILDA *appear up the stairs on the landing.* BASIL *knocks on the door*)

EDITH   Oh, that's Basil. Let him in, William.
   (WILLIAM *goes to the door.* JIMMIE *jumps up*)

JIMMIE I've got to change my shirt.

(*He exits to the bedroom.* WILLIAM *opens the door. He lets in* BASIL SMYTHE *and* HILDA ROSE. BASIL SMYTHE *is a short, untidy, rather plump man of fifty-some. He wears an old hat and a rather odd overcoat and has the unpredictable eccentric personality of the lonely. He carries an ungiftwrapped package and a large, fat somnolent cat with a collar and lead.* HILDA ROSE *is a rather smart minor-executive-type lady of forty-odd, with harlequin glasses and a rather racy, she hopes, manner. She has a large very fancily wrapped package*)

BASIL (*Panting*) Good evening, William. Many happy returns. I've brought Kitty.

WILLIAM Through all this slush?

BASIL She likes slush.

HILDA Hi, William.

WILLIAM Hello, Hilda. (*Pats the cat*) Hi, Kitty. My, you look spry.

HILDA I picked up this gentleman and his strange beast on the stairs. Pfu, it's Mount Everest, isn't it? Hi, Edith.

EDITH Hello, Hilda.

(HILDA *and* BASIL *start taking off their coats.* BASIL *gets into rather a tangle with the cat and the package*)

HILDA (*To* WILLIAM) Edith told me it was your birthday when she called to invite me. (*Sings*)
  "Happy birthday to you,
    Happy birthday to you,

13

Happy birthday, dear William,
Happy birthday to you."

WILLIAM   Thank you. It never seems like a birthday until someone sings.

BASIL   I don't know how she can sing after those stairs. I'm quite dizzy. (*Going into the living room still carrying the package and the cat*) Good evening, Edith. I understand you're the hostess. It was very kind of you to invite me. Oh, puff, puff.

EDITH   Are you all right, Basil?

BASIL   All right? Why wouldn't I be all right. Of course I'm all right. Say hello to Aunt Edith, Kitty.

EDITH   Isn't she a cute old something? (BASIL *puts the cat down*) Ronnie's coming specially for William's birthday.

BASIL   I'll believe in Ronnie's birthday present when I see it.

HILDA   (*Coming into the living room*)   Well, happy birthday to all, I say.

BASIL   I've brought you something, William. (*Presenting the package to* WILLIAM) I didn't know what to get so I got table mats.

WILLIAM   (*Taking the package*)   Thank you, Basil.
          (*As he starts to unwrap the pakage,* JIMMIE, *dressed, comes in from the bedroom*)

JIMMIE   Hello, hello, everyone. (*Seeing the cat*) My God, he's brought Pussikins. Is she still inheriting all your money, Basil? Or have you changed that will again?

BASIL (*Rather put out on seeing* JIMMIE) We're going to be five for bridge. We'll have to cut out.

JIMMIE Don't worry, Basil. You know I don't play. I'm going to the Philharmonic. (*Holding out a hand to* HILDA) Remember me? I'm Jimmie Luton.

HILDA Hello, Jimmie.

WILLIAM (*Holding up a blue place mat identical with the others*) Well. How charming.

BASIL I thought the other ones would be worn out by now.

WILLIAM They're not worn out at all. Look, I'm using them specially tonight for the occasion.

BASIL They were very good quality.

JIMMIE Now he's got twelve blue place mats.

HILDA (*Giving her present to* WILLIAM) It's just a gag, really, William. I saw it in the window at F. A. O. Schwartz. I thought maybe it would be good for a couple of laughs.

BASIL I think I've got heartburn from those stairs. (*Giving the cat to* JIMMIE) You hold Kitty. I wonder if I could have a drink of water, William. No, don't bother. I'll get it for myself.
    (BASIL *goes into the kitchenette*)

WILLIAM (*Unwrapping*) What can it be?

HILDA It's nothing. Absolutely nothing.
    (WILLIAM *unwraps the gift. It is a clockwork toy made of two fishes. When in operation, the large fish seems to be pursuing the little fish and finally swallows it*)

15

WILLIAM It's fascinating.

HILDA It's a fish.
(WILLIAM *puts it down*)

JIMMIE Watch out, for Chrissakes. Pussikins will have a stroke.
(*The toy works. They all stand watching as one fish
scurries after the other*)

BASIL (*Coming in from the kitchenette*) What's that?

WILLIAM It's a big fish swallowing a little fish.
(*The big fish swallows the little fish*)

BASIL A big fish swallowing a little fish. (*Takes the cat from*
JIMMIE) I call it sadistic. Don't you, Kitty? I'll take you
to the bedroom. (*Looks meaningfully at* HILDA) She hates
strangers.
(*He exits to the bedroom*)

JIMMIE Playing with toys at his age.

WILLIAM My second childhood began at twenty-seven.

EDITH It's real cute.

JIMMIE Well, who's going to have what, since I'm the barman? Hilda, a martini?

HILDA Gosh, it'll knock me out. But what the hell—celebrat-
ing. On the rocks, please.
(BASIL *returns from the bedroom*)

JIMMIE Okay. What about you, Basil? You're not drinking,
I suppose.

BASIL I never drink anything, you know that. But perhaps
since it's William's birthday, I'll toy with a little vermouth.

16

JIMMIE All right.
> (*He exits to the kitchenette.* HILDA *is inadvertently sitting in* BASIL's *special chair.* BASIL *eyes her with great disapproval*)

BASIL Excuse me.

HILDA (*Realizing, awkward*) Oh, pardon me.
> (*She rises.* BASIL *triumphantly seats himself in his chair*)

EDITH Well, everyone. Many happy returns to William.

HILDA What would we do without William?

BASIL I've known William thirty years. That's a great deal to William.

WILLIAM Too much I'm afraid.

BASIL Oh no, not at all. (*Sings*) "And it's never a day too much. There's not a person in the whole wide world who'd I'd change for my dear old Dutch."
> (*There is something a little wrong with this*)

HILDA (*Slightly embarrassed, to* EDITH) Have you seen Leon since we played bridge there?

EDITH No, I haven't.

HILDA Nor have I.

WILLIAM Nobody's seen Leon.

BASIL Which is very fortunate for them.

HILDA Well. So you don't like my good friend Leon Purson?

BASIL It's a very second-rate North Carolina family. Not one of the good North Carolina families. Not at all. And his aunt in Blowing Rock makes shocking headcheese.

JIMMIE (*Coming in with drinks; takes the martini to* HILDA *and the vermouth to* BASIL) Now there you are, Basil. Don't guzzle it.

BASIL I doubt whether I'll even touch it.

HILDA What cunning candles.

WILLIAM There, Jimmie. You've got a compliment.

JIMMIE It's about time. (*To* HILDA) Well, why are they leaving you standing about? (*Brings a chair*) Here you are, next to Basil.

(HILDA *sits next to a disapproving* BASIL)

BASIL Has anyone read *Girls Immured?* It's a paperback original. It's about girls in a reform school in Canada. It's very dirty. They're all Lesbians.

WILLIAM Not all of them. Surely, Basil.

BASIL What's the matter with that? These are sophisticated ladies. Edith has heard of Lesbians. I'm sure the other lady ... Helen ...

HILDA Hilda, thank you, sir.

BASIL I'm sure Hilda has heard of Lesbians, too. I don't mean to imply by that, of course, that she is one.

HILDA Really!

BASIL *Honi soit qui mal y pense.* Where there's smoke, there's fire.

HILDA (*To* JIMMIE) Have you read *Doctor Zhivago?*

BASIL It's too long.

HILDA I read it in the *Reader's Digest.* (*To* WILLIAM) Is this gentleman a great friend of yours?

WILLIAM Basil? A very great friend.

BASIL I've known William almost all my life. I've been mother and father to him. Though, of course, as it happens, I am a year younger than he is.

JIMMIE That's something new.

BASIL I graduated from Princeton summa cum laude in 1930, I moved to Philadelphia in 1932 and became a full partner in Parker and Lumb, one of the best publishing houses in the country. Of course, I've done a great many things since then and been in a great many places all over the world. I'm not doing very much now but that doesn't alter the fact that I'm very close to William. I love William. I'm going to leave him all my money in my will.

JIMMIE Did you hear that, Pussikins? Watch out.

EDITH (*Trying to cover*) The pussy willow isn't even out. It's extraordinary. I've never known such a late spring.

BASIL I've been very sick. I've had great bad luck with my health. That's what's made it all so—unmanageable. Am I talking too much, William dear?

WILLIAM Oh, no, Basil. Not at all.

JIMMIE It's living alone. That's what does it. Living with Kitty.

BASIL Kitty had a fur ball.

JIMMIE She's probably getting bald like me.

WILLIAM Well, we're all getting on. That's what birthday parties do for you. Remind you.

HILDA (*Annoyed*) I'm not getting that old, I'd have you know, sir.

EDITH And I don't live alone.

BASIL Neither does William. If he doesn't have you, he has the Lady from Philadelphia. William always spread himself very thin. Thank God I never did. Spread yourself thin and eventually you split.
 (*He sips the vermouth*)

HILDA Who's the Lady from Philadelphia?

JIMMIE My Lord, let's not go into her.

BASIL The Lady from Philadelphia is . . .

WILLIAM Basil, don't be a bore. This is meant to be my birthday party. (*Holding up his empty glass*) Jimmie, let's give them another martini.

JIMMIE Oh, all right. I suppose there's time.

BASIL (*Holding up his empty vermouth glass*) What about my vermouth?

JIMMIE (*Grabbing it*) Sipping!
 (*He exits to the kitchenette*)

BASIL The Lady from Philadelphia is a bitch, if you want to know the truth. A neurotic, useless, drunken old bitch who

plays on William like a succubus. Anyone but William . . .
I'm sorry, Edith dear. Is it indelicate to mention her in front
of you?

EDITH   Poor thing. That's all I think about her, Basil. She's
ruined her life. The poor old pitiful thing.

HILDA   You seem to be quite a Don Juan, William, if I can
believe your friends.

EDITH   Oh, it's just because William's so kind. He's kind to
everyone. Poor old thing, she's nothing now, living on a
pittance, getting drunk every night. But when William was
at Merton, she used to be a housemother or a matron. Wasn't
that what she was, William? A housemother? (*The front
door opens and* RONNIE JOHNSON *enters, carrying a smart suit-
case and wearing a smart overcoat. He is thirty-three, but
looks much younger, almost, on good days, boyish. He has a
crew-cut and a sort of breathless charm which comes from
nervous tension. In contrast to the others, he is "youth" and
"success," and to them he seems a very glamorous figure*)
Hello, Ronnie.

WILLIAM (*Delighted*)   Hi, Ronnie.

RONNIE   Hi, all. Where shall I dump my terrible bag, William?

WILLIAM   Anywhere. It doesn't matter. This is wonderful.
You're spending the night, aren't you?

EDITH   Everyone is, it seems.

RONNIE   Well, I was hoping I could, William. This is the only
place where I can get away from it all.

WILLIAM   Of course you're staying.

RONNIE Well, that's very hospitable of you.
(*He takes off his coat*)

WILLIAM This is triumphant. All my best friends. Now it really is a celebration.
(WILLIAM *comes with* RONNIE *into the living room*)

BASIL Good evening, my dear Ronnie.

RONNIE Oh, Basil, I didn't see you. How's Kitty?

BASIL She had a fur ball.

RONNIE I'll bet she's as buxom as ever.

BASIL She's considerably slimmer.

WILLIAM Ronnie—this is Hilda Rose. Hilda, this is my good friend Ronnie. He used to work in obscurity at the desk next to mine. Now he's the famous Ronnie Johnson.

HILDA Ronnie Johnson? *The Wasps of Salzburg?* Why, everyone was reading it last fall. Just everybody. My, am I thrilled to meet a real author.

RONNIE Hello. I'm still recovering from the New Haven and Hartford. It's the longest day's journey since O'Neill.

HILDA (*Titters sycophantically*) Oh, a bon mot already.

JIMMIE (*Coming out of the kitchenette with a cocktail shaker and another glass*) Well, well, the great man's arrived.

RONNIE Hello, Jimmie.

JIMMIE A civilized person at last.

BASIL Thank you.

JIMMIE And I've got William's extra ticket for the Phil-

22

harmonic. You're coming. That's all. Don't say a word. You're coming.

RONNIE I'm terribly sorry, Jimmie, but there's . . .

JIMMIE Oh, God, you and your conquests. The stallion of El Morocco. Why do they all adore you so much? You're spending the night, aren't you?

RONNIE Yes, I'm delighted to say.

JIMMIE I'm staying too. So you'll have the cot. But don't worry. It won't kill you.

RONNIE Nothing can kill me. I'm dead already.

WILLIAM What's the matter?

RONNIE That bastard book.

HILDA A new book? How thrilling.

RONNIE I'm in agony.

BASIL You fiddle too much. I've always told you. Good writers don't fiddle.

JIMMIE Poor boy, don't be beastly to him, Basil. Cheer up, Ronnie. Have a martini. I just fixed them this minute. You can't complain of ice water.

RONNIE I've never figured how you can fix drinks with you on the wagon.

JIMMIE I just remember the way I used to be. Brother! (*Pouring a martini and handing it to* RONNIE) There.

RONNIE Thanks. Oh, William, can I use your phone?

23

WILLIAM Of course. It's been missing you.

> (JIMMIE *starts pouring martinis for the others.* RONNIE *goes to the phone, lights a cigarette, and dials*)

EDITH (*From the kitchenette*) Get them to the table.

JIMMIE Drink up, ladies and gentlemen, dinner's almost ready.

RONNIE (*On phone, as they all studiously pretend not to listen*) Natasha? Angel, it's me. Listen, darling, I can't make it . . . No, not possibly. There's this terrible Stumpfig. You know him. My European publisher. Well, he thought he'd got Bill Clangdon to adapt that nauseous series of his but now at the last minute it looks as if Clangdon is precontracted. So you do see, don't you? (*As he hears this,* JIMMIE *grips* WILLIAM's *arm and indicates urgently that he should take action.* WILLIAM *pays no attention.* RONNIE *continues on the phone*) Yes, it's all fallen through. He's just got to find someone in a hurry and it's up to me to dazzle with a bright idea . . . Why me, darling? Because I'm so divinely selfless, wearing my fingers to the bone for others . . . That's why . . . Yes, sweetie, I know. I'm riven, but then we're always bumping into each other at somebody's monstrous party. Bye. Love, love, love—and to the Maestro.

> (*He hangs up*)

JIMMIE (*Pointedly*) What's all this about adaptations and translations, Ronnie?

RONNIE Oh, nothing. (*Moves away from the phone and trips over the toy on the floor*) What on earth is that?

HILDA A fish.

WILLIAM It's my birthday present from Hilda.

RONNIE   Your birthday? My God, I completely forgot. Or did I know? I'm sure I never knew. Oh, William, tell me I didn't know.

WILLIAM   I doubt whether it's going to make the world fall apart one way or the other.

RONNIE   But a birthday's a thing.

WILLIAM   A very tiny thing. I don't even know your birthday.

BASIL   Ronnie's birthday is June ninth.

RONNIE   Oh, Basil, you never forget anything, do you? Excuse me, William, may I brush my teeth?
(*He opens his bag and exits to the bathroom*)

EDITH   Well, if dinner's ready, I'd better go serve it. It's the least I can do, since it's meant to be my party. You sort everyone out, Jimmie. Hilda, would you light the candles?

HILDA   Love to, Edith.
(EDITH *exits to the kitchenette*)

JIMMIE   All right, everyone, *à table*. Bring up the chairs.
(*The two chairs between the table and the wall and the two chairs at either end are already in place. As everyone moves toward the table,* JIMMIE *and* WILLIAM *bring two more chairs and put them in the two remaining places, back to the audience.* RONNIE *returns*)

JIMMIE   (*As they all mill*)   Now, let me see. Edith sits by the kitchen, I suppose. I'll sit next to her. And then Hilda on the other side. No, Basil . . . And, Ronnie, since you're the guest of honor, you can have the great privilege of sitting opposite the birthday boy.

RONNIE But ... I'm sorry, Jimmie. There's been some mistake. I'm not staying for dinner.

JIMMIE But you've got to, for Chrissakes. It's all fixed. We're all expecting you.

RONNIE (*To* WILLIAM) William, this is terrible. I didn't realize ... I mean, when I called ... I can't. I just can't. There's this terrible Swiss. He's waiting for me right now, at the Plaza, probably cutting his throat. I feel awful, William, but there it is. I shouldn't even have waited for a drink. I've simply got to dash.
(*He picks up his coat. As he puts it on, all the others sit down in silence*)

BASIL (*Breaking the silence*) Am *I* going to see you at all this trip, Ronnie?

RONNIE What, Basil? Why, yes, of course. I'll call you in the morning. Maybe we can have lunch.

BASIL Call before nine. I don't like to be disturbed once I've started my research.

RONNIE Before nine. All right. Night, everyone. Night, William. Happy birthday.
(*He starts for the door.* EDITH *comes out of the kitchen-ette with the chicken, stares after the departing* RONNIE)

EDITH He's going? He isn't staying for dinner?

JIMMIE No.
(*The phone rings*)

RONNIE I'll take it. It's probably for me.

JIMMIE Why on earth should it be?

RONNIE I left the number.

> (RONNIE *runs to the telephone, lighting a cigarette. As he talks,* EDITH *brings the vegetables from the kitchen. She sits down.* JIMMIE *starts pouring the wine*)

RONNIE (*On phone*) Hello, Maggie . . . It's me . . . Look, I'm here and I'll see you, but I can't talk, not possibly. Not now . . . The Rockefellers? You poor sweetie but you'll live through it somehow. Love, love, love. (*He drops the receiver and dashes toward the door*) Thanks, William. (*He opens the door and goes.* WILLIAM *follows to the door*)

WILLIAM (*Calling after him*) Good-bye, Ronnie. Thanks for coming.

> (WILLIAM *returns to the table. They all sit, handing things in silence*)

BASIL (*Breaking the silence*) I could have told you, William. Ronnie wasting a New York evening with you? That would be the day.

> (*This only intensifies the silence. The dampened birthday party continues in silence. Suddenly* JIMMIE *jumps up*)

JIMMIE My God, I've forgotten the surprise! (*He dashes into the kitchenette*)

EDITH (*Trying*) It makes it much nicer with only five, doesn't it? It isn't so squashed.

HILDA (*Helping*) I hate being squashed at table. These *are* pretty red candles.

EDITH They're Portuguese. Portuguese altar candles.

HILDA   Someone around here has got exquisite taste and I wouldn't be surprised if it turned out to be William.

(JIMMIE *appears triumphantly in the kitchenette door, holding up a small loaf of French bread onto which he has stuck candles as on a birthday cake. The candles are lit*)

JIMMIE   *Voilà. La Grande Pièce de Résistance.* Why does it always have to be cake, anyway?

EDITH   My, it's cute, isn't it, William?

HILDA   And so original. I never saw anything like that before. Never.

(JIMMIE *puts the bread down on a small table for* WILLIAM *to blow out the candles*)

JIMMIE   Blow them out, William. You've got the strength. You're not that old.

(WILLIAM, *with his wine glass in his hand, crosses to the bread*)

WILLIAM   A loaf of bread, a jug of wine . . . (*Gestures back to the party at the table*) . . . and you.

(WILLIAM *blows out the candles. There are rather forced cries of approbation*)

JIMMIE (*Looking at his watch*)   My God, seven-thirty. The Egmont Overture.

(*He starts for the bedroom*)

EDITH   But, Jimmie, you can't go yet.

JIMMIE (*Going into the bedroom*)   Are you mad? And miss the Egmont Overture?

HILDA What's the Egmont Overture?

BASIL The overture to an opera called Egmont.

EDITH But, Jimmie, you haven't eaten.

JIMMIE (*Coming from the bedroom*) And thanks to whom? Who knew I was going to the Philharmonic and invited them for seven? (*Wildly searching his pockets*) The tickets. The goddam tickets. Wouldn't you know? (*He dashes back into the bedroom*)

HILDA My, there's a lot of movement around here tonight, isn't there?

EDITH (*Looking at the poppers that have been placed on the table*) Oh, let's pull that darling green one, Hilda.
(*They pull.* HILDA *gets it*)

JIMMIE (*Rushing out of the bedroom*) Good-bye, good-bye, all. (*As he passes the seated* WILLIAM, *he pats his head*) Happy birthday, William.
(WILLIAM *rises and follows him to the door*)

WILLIAM (*Calling*) Have a good time, Jimmie.
(WILLIAM *closes the door and comes back to sit at the table.* HILDA *has discovered a paper hat in the popper and holds it up to show* EDITH. BASIL, *who has been eating, totally disinterested, sees the hat*)

BASIL I like that hat. I want that hat.
(*He snatches the hat from* HILDA, *puts it on his head rather wrong, and continues eating*)

EDITH Now we must get a hat for William.
(*She holds a popper to* WILLIAM, *who helps her pop it.*

HILDA *throws a streamer. But in spite of these efforts, the birthday party isn't coming off.* RONNIE's *desertion, and then* JIMMIE's, *has made them all feel suddenly dull and unwanted and elderly*)

WILLIAM (*Rises and lifts his glass*) Let us drink to us. We're all very fascinating people. (*To* HILDA) A lady executive. (*To* BASIL, *who goes on eating*) A distinguished ex-publisher. (*To* EDITH) American womanhood at its peak. (*To himself*) And yours truly, William Baker.

The Curtain Falls

The same—around 2:45 A.M. The dining table has not been cleared. The bedroom door is closed. In the center of the stage is a bridge table with the huntsmen-shaded lamp pulled up to it.

At rise, WILLIAM, BASIL, HILDA *and* EDITH *are seated at the table, playing bridge. They all have drinks and are smoking.* JIMMIE, *with his jacket off, is lying on the daybed reading* The Possessed. WILLIAM *is benignly drunk, with only the slightest hint of desperation behind it.* BASIL, *with a glass of beer, is very fuddled.*

BASIL (*Very loud, having lost control of his voice*) I was the making of that boy. He came to me with his first book when I was chief editor at Murchison's.

WILLIAM Play, Basil.

BASIL I am playing, and I read the manuscript and I said, Mr. Johnson, Ronnie, if I may call you that since I'm almost old enough to be your father—Ronnie, I'm not sure, I'm not completely sure, I may be wrong, there is always that possibility, but I think you have written a masterpiece. It wasn't, of course. And he never came anywhere near to it after he switched to Harper's. (*Sips beer and hiccups*) Excuse me. Hic.

WILLIAM (*Taking the last trick*) There we are, partner. Five shiny spades. To dig with.

EDITH   Game and rubber.

WILLIAM   What do you know? The invisible—I mean, the invincible—William Baker has done it again.

BASIL   He hasn't been good to me, that boy. I don't want to be acrimonious in any way, but he won't call me tomorrow. I'm here to tell you. That boy won't call me for lunch. And I have a credit card at Longchamps. Oh dear, hic again.

WILLIAM   (*Calling*)   Jimmie.

JIMMIE   Oh, so you're deigning to recognize my existence, are you?

WILLIAM   Drinks for everyone, barman. Freshen up.

JIMMIE   For Chrissakes, William, do you realize what time it is? Three o'clock almost. Do you want to be late again and have that little bastard Lexy Potter calling up at two minutes past nine? Bawling you out as if you were his scrub lady or something?

EDITH   He can have one more rubber on his birthday.

JIMMIE   It isn't his birthday any more. He's been a pumpkin for three hours.

WILLIAM   Not a pumpkin—a mouse. I'm not the coach. I'm one of the horses. Giddyap.

HILDA   It is getting kind of late, William. Terribly cute party but I'm for Tailored Woman tomorrow at the witching hour of nine.

WILLIAM   Nobody wants just one more rubber—for the road?

BASIL Let the poor woman go. She's probably got a sexual rendezvous.

HILDA Well, really!

BASIL What's the matter with that? I didn't say it was a sexual rendezvous with a Lesbian, did I?

HILDA (*Getting up*) I'm leaving. Can I have my things, William?

WILLIAM Now, Hilda, don't be mad at Basil. Remember all the weight of experience that lies behind his smallest utterances.

EDITH (*Totting up*) At least wait till I've figured up the score.

BASIL Everybody has to have the right sexual rhythm. Kinsey found that out. Kinsey or someone. It is a well-known scientific fact. Everybody has to have his or her own particular sexual rhythm. Now, with me I find it's exactly one point seven times a week.

EDITH (*Totting up*) William, you win everything. Can you beat that? How marvelous.

JIMMIE Marvelous William winning at bridge! When he could have gone to the Philharmonic. What a marvelous way to use valuable time. How marvelous not to waste it like me, reading *The Possessed*. (HILDA, *searching in her bag for change, giggles*) Or trying to read *The Possessed* through all this cackle and shouting.

BASIL *The Possessed* is too long. It's the exact sexual rhythm. Not one point six, not one point eight . . .

33

HILDA   For Pete's sake, Edith, how much do I owe, so I can get out of this nuthouse?

WILLIAM   Now, Hilda, graciousness at all times.

EDITH   (*Finished with her totting*)   It's seventy-three cents, Hilda. To William. Basil, a dollar to William. And I'm absolutely even. Quits.

BASIL   (*Fumbling in his pocket*)   Always pay your bridge debts on the nose—right on the nose. My father always said that. My father was a scholar and a gentleman. (*Produces a dollar and puts it on the table*)   There, William dear. One point seven . . .

HILDA   (*Slams down three quarters*)   To hell with the two cents change. William, thank you, thank you, kind sir. A lovely party.

BASIL   If you're going my way, I'll drop you off in my taxi.

HILDA   Me? In a taxi with you? Are you out of your mind?

BASIL   (*Meek*)   I only thought if you were going my way . . . Hic . . .

HILDA   And get my bottom pinched one point seven times. Ugh, dirty old man. (*She hurries into the hall.* WILLIAM *starts to follow her but she runs out of the apartment*)

WILLIAM   (*Calling loudly down the stairs*)   Hey, Hilda. Hilda.

EDITH   Sh, you'll wake everybody up.

WILLIAM   (*Coming back*)   Well, that's too bad.

BASIL   What's the matter with her?

34

WILLIAM   She wasn't used to you, Basil. That's all.

EDITH   And you do take some getting used to.

JIMMIE   What a cow. My God, Edith, couldn't you have found someone less dreary for William's birthday? (*Imitating*) Thank you, kind sir. For Chrissakes.

BASIL   I only said that Kinsey said . . . Where's Kitty?

JIMMIE   Don't you remember? In the bedroom. Taking a nap. Lucky Kitty.
        (*He exits into the bedroom for the cat*)

WILLIAM   Basil, are you all right? You're sure you can get home all right?

EDITH   It's cleared up now. You'll get a taxi all right.

BASIL   Of course I'm all right. I'm always all right. Why wouldn't I be all right? Kitty will be furious, though. She hates staying out so late. Good night, Edith. You're a very efficient woman.
        (*He kisses her*)

EDITH   Good night, Basil.

JIMMIE   (*Coming in from the bedroom with the cat*)   Here's the Bride of Frankenstein.
        (BASIL *and* WILLIAM *go into the hall.* JIMMIE *follows with the cat.* BASIL *is very unsteady.* WILLIAM *helps* BASIL *on with his coat.* JIMMIE *gives him the cat*)

BASIL   I'm sorry, William. I didn't mean to make that woman mad.

35

WILLIAM   That's all right, Basil. I thought you were very amusing.

BASIL   People are so irascible. I despise irascible people. Look at Leon's impossible attitude about that headcheese. Whatever he says and whoever he claims made it, it was distinctly rancid. I hope it'll never be my misfortune to see Leon Purson again—ever. And I thought he was my friend. Well, many happy returns of the day, William. Should auld acquaintance be forgot? No, no, never. I'll have to be up at the crack of dawn. So much research. I hope Kitty doesn't get another fur ball. Well, good night, William dear.

WILLIAM and JIMMIE   Good night, Basil.

BASIL   I think my heartburn's coming back.
   (BASIL *goes out the front door.* WILLIAM *shuts it and, followed by* JIMMIE, *returns to the living room, where* EDITH *is still straightening*)

JIMMIE (*It occurs to him*)   For Chrissakes, you didn't put the chain on the door.

WILLIAM   Ronnie's going to come.

JIMMIE   Never mind about Ronnie. I'll hear him. I'll let him in. (*Goes to the door and puts the chain on*) I don't care about you and Edith, but I'm not going to be murdered in my bed.

EDITH   I do wish Basil would forget about that headcheese. Lucky he's got all that money. Without that money he'd be in the gutter.

JIMMIE   Or dead. Everyone of his organs must have fungus on it.

36

WILLIAM   Poor Basil, it's sad—so sad.

JIMMIE   Of course, it's sad. But you dote on it, don't you? Poor
Basil, he's got nobody, he's an old drunk, he lives alone with a
cat. Kind wonderful William being St. Francis to the downtrodden.

EDITH   Oh, just shut up, will you, Jimmie?

JIMMIE   Shut up? Me?

EDITH   You've been picking on William all evening and it's
his birthday. Put the bridge table away and get out the cot
for Ronnie.

JIMMIE   Oh, all right. A beast of burden. That's all I am
around here. (*Takes the bridge table to the hall, grumbling*)
I'm not going to put it in the closet. Not with that goddam
cot. (*Pulling the folded cot out of the closet*) Come on, cot.
Come on out, ghastly stinky old cot.

EDITH   Why do you let him pick on you all the time? William,
I just don't understand.

WILLIAM   Jimmie's all right.

JIMMIE   (*Hearing his name mentioned*)   What are you saying
about me?

WILLIAM   I said since you're so exhausted you'd better use the
bathroom first.

JIMMIE   (*Rolling the cot into the living room*)   I used it hours
ago. Don't you think I have any sense? Edith, you get in it,
for God's sake . . . so we can all get a little sleep.

EDITH   I like getting into my robe first. You go, William. I'll get into my blue robe.

(*She starts for the bedroom*)

WILLIAM   Blue, blue as the sea where, proudly cutting through the foam, skims the *S.S. Pastores.*

JIMMIE (*Calling to* EDITH)   Hey, wait a minute. I've got to get my pillow out of there.

EDITH (*As she exits to the bedroom*)   Well, can't you be in the bedroom alone with me for a minute? Will you faint or something?

(JIMMIE *follows her into the bedroom.* WILLIAM, *alone, finds* HILDA's *half-finished drink and picks it up*)

JIMMIE (*Coming in with a pillow*)   You and your women. Thank God we've been spared the Lady from Philadelphia again. What happened, do you suppose? Passed out, I suppose. (*Seeing the drink in* WILLIAM's *hand*)   William, that's Hilda's drink. You're drinking Hilda's drink.

WILLIAM   Waste not, want not. A drink in time saves nine.

JIMMIE   Drink, bridge. Time passing all the time. Precious time. And what do you do? Deaden yourself, stupefy yourself. (WILLIAM *goes into the bathroom.* JIMMIE, *starting to undress and scattering his clothes about, follows to a spot near the hall from which he can go on talking to* WILLIAM *in the bathroom. As he undresses*)   I'm reading *The Possessed.* Greatest novel ever written. I'm rereading it. That's what I'm doing and, by God, even if you don't get everything, it's good, it nourishes you. You used to play the piano. Brahms' Intermezzi. Remember how well you played? Do you keep it up? Where's your piano even? You gave it to the Lady from Philadelphia because she needed something to put her rubber plant on. And now there's that Swiss publisher, desperate for someone—and what do you do? You're dying, dying, dying. You're letting yourself die. (*The toilet flushes in the bathroom*) Oh, what's the use. (*He is undressed down to his undershirt and shorts. He goes to the daybed, tosses the big bolster cushions onto a chair, pulls back the clothes and climbs in. He picks up* The Possessed *and starts to read. He hums a theme from the Egmont Overture*) Egmont.

    (EDITH *comes out of the bedroom in a blue negligee. She is carrying a pillow. She comes over to* JIMMIE)

EDITH   You've got my pillow.

JIMMIE   Your pillow? For Chrissakes, it's my pillow.

EDITH   No, it's my special pillow. Here. Take this.
    (*She tosses the pillow onto the bed and tugs the other pillow out from under* JIMMIE)

JIMMIE   For Chrissakes.
    (WILLIAM *comes out of the bathroom with his shirt off, still carrying the drink*)

WILLIAM   Well, I didn't take long, did I? A little toothpaste— a little mouthwash—and good-bye, birthday.

EDITH   Jimmie took my special pillow.
    (*She crosses to* WILLIAM, *kisses him and goes into the bathroom, leaving the pillow with* WILLIAM)

WILLIAM   You shouldn't have taken her pillow.

JIMMIE   That's right. Go on about her pillow. That's frightfully important, isn't it? Her pillow. I suppose it's the first pillow you ever crumpled together on the *S.S. Pastores*. My

God, I wish Ronnie would come back. I wish there'd be at least someone to have a civilized conversation with.

WILLIAM (*The drunkenness is showing pretty much now*) It happens to be her pillow because she likes a dacron pillow.
(*The phone rings*)

JIMMIE There, you see, the Lady from Philadelphia hasn't passed out.

WILLIAM Maybe it's Ronnie.

JIMMIE No, no, Ronnie wouldn't call at this hour. If he comes back, he comes back. If he doesn't, he doesn't. It's her.

WILLIAM Let's be grammatical, professor. It's *she*. But it isn't actually she who's making that din, is it? It's only the Bell Telephone Company. Ring out wild Bell Telephone Company.

JIMMIE And have her keep us awake all night?

WILLIAM She can call as much as she likes. She's my friend, my old, old friend. She was the only one at Merton who stood by me. If she wants to, she can call till the crack of doom.

EDITH (*Coming out of the bathroom*) The phone's ringing, William.

JIMMIE Is it?

EDITH Oh, it's the Lady from Philadelphia. You're not going to answer it, are you, William?

WILLIAM (*Goes to phone and picks it up*) Viola, hi, Viola . . . Oh, she's hung up. Probably the dog started scratching and she got distracted.

EDITH Poor pitiful old thing. Come to bed, darling. Good night, Jimmie.

WILLIAM   Good night, Jimmie.

JIMMIE   Oh, go to hell. (WILLIAM *and* EDITH *go into the bedroom and close the door.* JIMMIE *gets up from the bed and trips over the toy*)Goddam fish. (JIMMIE *picks up the toy and puts it on the table. He goes back to the bed, gets into it, then out of it again. He kneels down in a childish attitude of prayer*) Dear God, thank you for the blessings of this day and thank you for your over-all blessings, not that they're anything special. At least Bernice Weinstock has a certain talent in art class. At least she responds. At least there's a glimmer of understanding somewhere. That's a blessing and thank you, God. (*The carillon of the church chimes*) Bastard church. But most of all, thank you for William. I know he only puts up with me. But at least if you've got someone or a bit of someone, it nourishes. It makes it easier to fight for the finer, better things. It helps to nourish . . . (*The door opens quietly and then clatters against the chain.* JIMMIE *jumps up*) My God . . . Ronnie, is that you? . . . Is that you, Ronnie?

RONNIE   (*Off*)   This impossible chain.

JIMMIE   It's all right. Wait a minute. (JIMMIE *goes to the door, removes the chain, and opens to* RONNIE) I thought you were the marauder.

        (RONNIE *takes off his coat.* JIMMIE *puts the chain back*)

RONNIE   I woke you up. How terrible. I'm so sorry.

JIMMIE   You didn't awaken me. The party's only just over.

RONNIE   Where's William?

JIMMIE   In bed with Edith.

RONNIE (*Takes off his jacket*)   Am I dead!

JIMMIE   Are you drunk? Everyone else is except me.

RONNIE   I'm sort of drunk. My teeth.

JIMMIE   What?

RONNIE   I'm going to the bathroom to brush my teeth while I still have them. I've got a dentist date tomorrow. He'll probably pull them all out.

JIMMIE   Okay. Oh, my God.

RONNIE   What's the matter?

JIMMIE   I forgot to get the stuff for the cot. I'll have to disturb them.

RONNIE   Why?

JIMMIE   The sheets and things. I left them in a pile in the bedroom.

RONNIE   Well, I've got to brush my teeth.
(*He exits to the bathroom.* JIMMIE *crosses to the bedroom door and hesitates outside it*)

JIMMIE (*Calling softly*)   William? William?

WILLIAM (*Opens the door and salutes*)   Aye, aye, sir.

JIMMIE   Ronnie's back. I forgot to make up the cot. I need the sheets and blankets.

WILLIAM (*Goes back into the bedroom*)   For God's sake.

JIMMIE   Excuse me, Edith. (WILLIAM *comes out carrying a pile of sheets and blankets. He shuts the door behind him*) Don't pretend you were asleep just to make me feel bad.

It isn't possible. You've only been in there a couple of minutes.
(*He tries to take the bundle*)

WILLIAM   No, I'll do it.

JIMMIE   You don't have to.

WILLIAM   I'm the host. I make up my guests' beds.
(*Together they open the cot and start putting on the sheets and blankets*)

JIMMIE   Is she mad?

WILLIAM   Who?

JIMMIE   Edith. Who do you think I meant, for Chrissakes?

WILLIAM   How do I know whether she's mad or not.

JIMMIE   Were you doing it?

WILLIAM   Don't be romantic.

JIMMIE   I thought maybe on your birthday . . .

RONNIE   (*Appearing at the bathroom door, brushing his teeth*)
Good morning.
(*He exits back to the bathroom*)

WILLIAM   Is Ronnie drunk?

JIMMIE   He says he is, but he always says that. I don't think he is.

WILLIAM   Ronnie never gets drunk.

JIMMIE   It's because he sees interesting people, does interesting things. Ronnie's alive every minute of the day.

WILLIAM   That's because he's young.

JIMMIE   That's all it is? Just because you're young? You can't be alive if you're not young?

WILLIAM   Hospital corners—puleeze.

JIMMIE   He isn't that young, for Chrissakes. Young compared to us maybe.
   (RONNIE *comes out of the bathroom in pajamas*)

RONNIE   William, why on earth are you doing that?

WILLIAM   I'm making your bed. Jimmie's supposed to be helping.

JIMMIE   I am helping, William.

RONNIE   But it's mad. I can do it.

JIMMIE   Helpless little you? I bet you couldn't even boil an egg.

WILLIAM   (*Finishing the bed*)   There. That's it. What about a nightcap, Ronnie?

JIMMIE   Don't you do it, Ronnie. He just wants another drink himself. Don't you let him get away with it.

WILLIAM   Not just a teeny-weeny little nightcap?

RONNIE   (*Getting into the cot*)   Father William, I'm never going to drink again. There isn't any milk, is there?

WILLIAM   Milk, for God's sake.

JIMMIE   You know Ronnie always likes his milk, William.
   (WILLIAM *goes into the kitchenette and turns on the light.*

Martin Gabel and Jason Robards, Jr., as WILLIAM BAKER and BASIL SMYTHE

JIMMIE *is sitting on his bed, eager for news of the "glamour" world*) You had a perfectly ghastly time as usual, I suppose.

RONNIE Lousy. That terrible Swiss and then some lethal party. (WILLIAM *comes from the kitchenette with milk*)

WILLIAM Here you are.

RONNIE (*Taking it*) Cheers.

JIMMIE Who was at the party?

RONNIE Oh, the same as usual. Everyone.

JIMMIE Everyone being brilliant, I bet. My, you certainly lead a life. What about your Swiss friend? Did he get the man he wanted?

RONNIE No, it's completely fallen through.

JIMMIE Did you think of someone else?

RONNIE A total blank.

JIMMIE Then, Ronnie, I wonder . . .

WILLIAM (*Breaking in quickly*) For God's sake, do you know what time it is? Ronnie, do you have to get up in the morning?

RONNIE (*Drinking milk*) God, yes. Dentist at nine-thirty. I'm always going to the dentist, aren't I? Soon you won't believe I have a tooth left in my head. But I do.
(*He flashes his teeth*)

WILLIAM Then I'll wake you when I get up?

RONNIE I'll probably hit you, but yes, please.

JIMMIE I've got to get up too, for God's sake. I've got to get back to my girls in the suburbs. Ugh!

EDITH (*Calling from the bedroom*) William? What on earth's the matter? What are you doing?

WILLIAM (*Furtively pouring himself a drink*) Nothing else you want, Ronnie?

RONNIE No thanks, William.

WILLIAM Then good night.

RONNIE Good night, William.

EDITH (*Calling*) William!
(WILLIAM *hesitates and then, taking the drink with him, goes toward the bedroom*)

WILLIAM I am coming, my own, my love, be it ever so dainty a tread.

JIMMIE (*Noticing the drink for the first time*) William, you took another drink.
(WILLIAM *shuts the bedroom door behind him*)

RONNIE Wouldn't you if you were going to sleep with Edith?

JIMMIE He shouldn't. It's bad for him. He'll feel terrible in the morning.
(RONNIE *takes a last sip of milk, yawns.* JIMMIE *turns out the remaining light by his bed and gets into the bed. For a moment all is silence. Then* JIMMIE *gets out of bed and turns the light on again*)

JIMMIE Ronnie.

RONNIE (*Sleepy*) Yes.

JIMMIE I know you're dying to go to sleep, but there's something—something important. Can I talk to you?

RONNIE (*Not pleased*) I'm all ears. Every inch of me is ears.

JIMMIE It's about William. Do you think he's a bore? You don't, I know, because if you did you wouldn't always stay here when you come to New York. (*Pause*) Or is it because it's so near Grand Central?

RONNIE Jimmie—really.

JIMMIE But don't you ever think about him, buried in that goddam textbook publishing company. Don't you think he's capable of more, much more than that?

RONNIE I always think of William the way he is, plodding along, mothering his lame ducks, servicing his two fearful consorts.

JIMMIE But didn't you see him tonight? Drunk as a lord. He's that way most every night. He just doesn't care whether he lives or dies. It's been that way ever since Merton. And he was the youngest full professor they ever had. Brilliant, absolutely brilliant. Everyone said he'd be the next president of the college.

RONNIE Didn't they fire him or something?

JIMMIE Bastards.

RONNIE What was it all about?

JIMMIE You don't know, do you?

47

RONNIE   I haven't the remotest idea.

JIMMIE   Nobody does, practically, except me. Maybe if I told you . . .

RONNIE   Tell, tell.

JIMMIE   You must swear never to let anyone know—especially William.

RONNIE   Of course.

JIMMIE   Well, there was a student in his junior biology class. A monstrous little rich girl with a meat-packing father and a face like a Hormel ham. She was crazy about William, flopping all over him night and day. And William, being William, just trying to be kind—My God, even King Farouk wouldn't have touched her—used to have her for tea, listen to her girlish dilemmas, try to straighten her out. That's all. That's absolutely all. And then one night she got into William's apartment, took his razor and slashed her wrists. The little bitch.

RONNIE   She killed herself?

JIMMIE   And left a note. It accused William of God knows what.

RONNIE   Wow.

JIMMIE   William never even touched her. She must have been raving mad. But would the bastards believe him? In a pig's eye. They made him leave in the middle of the semester; obviously he could never work in a college again. And it broke him. I'd have fought. I'd have torn their fat bellies off with my nails. But not William. He just gave up. He came to New York, got that job, where they were willing to hire him. And that was that.

RONNIE   Poor William, poor old Father William.

JIMMIE   If only there was something new, something stimulating . . .

RONNIE   My God, why don't I get him the job with Stumpfig?

JIMMIE   Oh, could you, could you?

RONNIE   It never even entered my head.

JIMMIE   He's got everything.

RONNIE   Of course I could. Why not? Yes, why not? Maybe all sorts of birds could be killed. (*Yawns*) Let's sleep on it, Jimmie.

JIMMIE   Gosh, I'd be grateful.

RONNIE   Grateful enough to turn off that light?

JIMMIE   I'm sorry. (*Turns off the light*) You'll never let him know I talked about Merton, will you?

RONNIE   Never, never, never, never, never. *King Lear,* Act Five. Good night, Jimmie.

JIMMIE   Good night. (*There is a pause*) There'd be quite a lot of money, wouldn't there?

RONNIE   What?

JIMMIE   Money.

RONNIE   Oh, sure.

JIMMIE   Are you asleep?

RONNIE   Oh no, I'm wide awake.

JIMMIE   I've been reading up about islands—islands in the Caribbean. It's a dream I've got and now maybe it could come true. One day I'll be retiring and so will William . . . and on some of those islands you can still live cheap . . . With my pension and all the money William's going to make and our social security . . . we wouldn't need much. Just a few books, the best books, the sun, the sea pounding on the silver sand, and some fishing lines, I guess, and . . . no Edith . . . (*The phone rings*)   No goddam Lady from Philadelphia.

RONNIE (*Startled awake by the phone*)   At this hour?

JIMMIE   At any hour.
      (*The phone rings again*)

RONNIE   Aren't you going to answer it?

JIMMIE   Me? If she knew I was here she'd be over in a helicopter with a carving knife! She's jealous of all William's friends. She's even jealous of me. Can you imagine? It's like being jealous of Dame May Whitty.
      (*The phone continues to ring. Both* JIMMIE *and* RONNIE *are lying in bed. The bedroom door opens and* WILLIAM *comes sleepily to answer the phone*)

WILLIAM (*Softly*)   Pardon me, friends. (*He picks up the phone and speaks with great sweetness and comfort*)   Hello, Viola. How sweet of you to call. How's the dog? . . . Oh, I'm sorry, but use that salve the vet gave you. That'll stop the scratching . . . Sure, Viola, everything's okay, just fine . . . Look,

Viola, you've had a couple of drinks and so have I. So off to bed, okay? ... Get your rest ... I'll see you soon ... sure ... sure ... Now, Viola, you know I'm always here. You know I'll never go away ... Of course, Viola, I'd have been terribly disappointed if you hadn't called to say Happy Birthday.

The Curtain Falls

ACT TWO

SCENE ONE

The same—8:30 the next morning. WILLIAM, *dressed except for his jacket, is coming out of the kitchenette with a glass of orange juice. His jacket is on the back of a chair.* RONNIE *is still asleep in the cot.*

WILLIAM (*Stooping and shaking* RONNIE'S *shoulder*) Wake up, Ronnie. Orange juice.

JIMMIE (*Appearing from the hall in a robe, with another robe over his arm*) Wake up, for Chrissakes. Get cracking, man. We're late. Everybody's late. It's almost eight-thirty.
  (*He stands hovering tensely by the bed*)

RONNIE (*Groans, stirs in bed, looks up at* WILLIAM) Hello, William.

WILLIAM Good morning. You said you wanted to get up.

RONNIE Oh, God!

WILLIAM Orange juice. It has to be faced.

RONNIE (*Sitting up, grabbing the orange juice, gulping it*) How do you feel?

WILLIAM Fine and dandy.

RONNIE How do you do it? I feel like the entire personnel of the House of Usher.

WILLIAM There's coffee almost ready and English muffins coming up.

RONNIE In *that* toaster?

WILLIAM It's simple if you know how.
(*He goes into the kitchenette*)

JIMMIE Here's one of William's robes. You never bring a
robe. Don't you even own one, for Chrissakes? I thought
authors lived in dressing gowns. (*Throws the robe on the
bed and hisses conspiratorially*) You're going to talk to him,
aren't you? You promised. I'll keep out of the way. (*Loud,
for* WILLIAM) I'm going to get the bathroom over—*if* there's
any hot water.

WILLIAM (*Coming out of the kitchenette with two cups of
coffee*) There isn't any.
(JIMMIE *groans and exits to the bathroom*)

RONNIE (*Getting up, putting on the robe*) God help my dentist. When I open my mouth, he'll turn to stone. Why can't
I get up in the morning?

WILLIAM (*Putting the cups of coffee down on the table*) Here.
It's only instant, I'm afraid.

RONNIE (*Sitting down at the table*) Is it true that Edith calls
it inst?

WILLIAM (*Sitting down*) Yes.

RONNIE I don't believe it.

WILLIAM It's one of the joys of my life.

RONNIE (*Gulps the coffee*) I don't feel any better.

WILLIAM Poor Ronnie.

RONNIE Jimmie's in the bathroom, isn't he?

56

WILLIAM   He'll be there for hours. It's his scalp.

RONNIE   Then we can talk.

WILLIAM   Talk?

RONNIE   If we're capable of talking, which I doubt. William, I've got what I think is a wonderful idea. It could be terrible, of course. All ideas can always be either. (*Gulps the coffee*) I couldn't have some sugar, could I?

WILLIAM   Oh, I forgot you take sugar. I . . . No, look, there's some on the table in my mother's thing.

RONNIE   Thank God for your mother's thing. (*Takes a piece of sugar out of a little silver sugar rack and drops it in his coffee. Looks for a spoon. There isn't one. Tries to stir the coffee with his finger. It is too hot*) Ouch! (*Gets up and goes into the kitchenette and comes out with a spoon*) I can always find spoons. I'm a sort of Geiger counter for spoons. (*Sits down, stirs the coffee*) I was talking to Jimmie last night. Edith's still asleep, isn't she?

WILLIAM   Yep.

RONNIE   And I gather you're not completely happy in your job.

WILLIAM   (*Defensive*)   I can't imagine why he said that.

RONNIE   Well, he didn't say it exactly. It's just that . . . I mean, well, Lexy Potter is pretty much of a bastard and there's not much future and . . . What the hell is the point? Oh, yes, I know. If something else came up, something that could be quite exciting . . . would you maybe consider it?

WILLIAM   It's rather a hypothetical question, isn't it?

57

RONNIE   My God, would I be asking hypothetical questions at this hour? You know what I'm driving at, don't you?

WILLIAM   Well ... yes ... I think I do.

RONNIE   Even when I knew Paul Stumpfig was desperate, it never occurred to me. Can you believe it? And then suddenly I thought, Why not William? William's got a hell of a lot of talent.

WILLIAM   Not any more.

RONNIE   William, do try to be a little less Chekhov or I'll throw up in your mother's thing.

WILLIAM   But it's true. I find I forget things. I lose things. I hear myself saying the same thing over and over again. I'm getting old.

RONNIE   That isn't age. It's rust ... barnacles.

WILLIAM   I don't forget facts. Nothing like that. And I keep up with the new findings in biology. It's just that—well, I lose keys. I forget to buy groceries. I forget whether bridge is meant to be at my house or someone else's.

RONNIE   Holy Mother of God. Do you remember when I was working at the office and you started translating that novel from the French?

WILLIAM   I never finished it.

RONNIE   But it was beautifully done. And it was amusing doing it, wasn't it? Much more stimulating than servicing middle-aged ladies and playing interminable whist.

WILLIAM   I enjoyed fiddling around with it very much.

RONNIE So scrape off the barnacles. Face the fact that life can be beautiful and begin at eighty and be positive and all that crap. It really can and it's idiotic to snub it just because all those Norman Vincent Fosdicks are so vomititious. I'm really getting terribly carried away by the idea. Don't you want to hear what it involves?

WILLIAM Yes, I want to hear.

RONNIE Then listen. This Swiss, Paul Stumpfig, my European publisher. He's a dreadful old bore but he's one of my dearest friends. And he's a terribly slick guy. He's going to be really big in international publishing and ... (*Abundant smoke is pouring out of the kitchenette*) My God, that toaster.

WILLIAM (*Jumping up*) For God's sake. (*He runs into the kitchenette*)

RONNIE Simple if you know how!

WILLIAM (*Coming back*) The muffins have passed away. Shall I start some more?

RONNIE William, we're settling your whole future. We don't need English muffins for that. Really, it's like trying to talk to a moron. Sit down. (WILLIAM *sits down*. RONNIE *coughs*) Anyone would think you'd been burning Joan of Arc in there. Well, the whole idea's wildly ambitious—a series of cheap books on contemporary subjects. They're distributing them all over the world in almost every language to educate the lovely thinking masses of today. Millions of copies, literally. But the whole thing's going up in smoke ... (*Coughs*) ... if you'll pardon the expression, because the editor Paul hired to supervise the texts was no good. When he flew over he thought he'd got Bill Clangdon. You know, that smart-ass journalist who's always writing: Be Glad You're a Leper.

WILLIAM And now Clangdon won't do it?

RONNIE He can't. He's mad for it, but he's precontracted. (*Coughs again*) My God, who would have thought the old bun had so much smoke in it?
  (JIMMIE *bursts out of the bathroom with a towel on his head*)

JIMMIE William, William, something's on fire. Smoke's pouring through the bathroom wall.

WILLIAM It's only the toaster again.

JIMMIE Oh! (*Looks conspiratorially at* RONNIE *and smiles, pleased*) Oh, well, maybe it'll cure my scalp like Hickory smoked ham.
  (*He goes back into the bathroom*)

RONNIE Well, William, are you interested?

WILLIAM Ronnie, I don't know what to say.

RONNIE I hate people saying things. I only like the things I say myself.

WILLIAM I've always admired you very much, you know.

RONNIE Oh, *merde*. Who got me started?

WILLIAM It's true. When you came to the office, it had been so long since I'd met anyone exceptional. You brought—well, a sort of zest. Before you came—years before—I'd decided that ambition and I had parted company once and for all. But when I met you and watched your career . . .

RONNIE Bless you, Father William, but this is hardly the moment for the stories of our lives. So is it a deal?

WILLIAM But they wouldn't consider me, would they?

RONNIE With me sponsoring you? Are you crazy? My God, the first book's on biology, too. *The Sperm and You*. And brother, what you don't know about the sperm!

WILLIAM (*For a long moment, he says nothing*) But, Ronnie, it's been so long. You talked about rust. I'm corroded in it. And it isn't just that.

RONNIE William, listen to me. Bad things may have happened to you. I don't know. I don't know a thing about it. But if they did, they're dead and gone. You're not even the same person. Every seven years you change every cell in your body. You're a biologist. You know that. Join Paul and me for lunch. Pavillon at one. Okay?

WILLIAM Yesterday, when you called from Grand Central, I must admit I did have one mad moment. But I came down to earth soon because . . . well, I know what I am and I knew you'd seen me day after day, sitting at the second desk from the window, plodding along, doing Lexy Potter's dirty work. And I didn't think, I didn't even dream that you'd give me a thought and . . .
    (*His voice trails off*)

RONNIE William, William. That's right. Let's get a little choky. It's a good sign. It hits where you need to be hit. You can do it. Ronnie Johnson is talking and Ronnie J. knows everything and Ronnie J. says you can do it.

WILLIAM Where's Pavillon?

RONNIE Ah, Judas, there's a symptom of atrophy by barnacle. The Ritz Tower.
> (*He salutes smartly*)

WILLIAM I don't see why I couldn't do it. I have the languages. I can write. I do know quite a bit, enough. But you don't think your friend will feel I'm a bit—senior?

RONNIE My God, Old Cancer-Can-Be-Joyous Clangdon is ninety-five if he's a day. You'll be a mere slip of a boy. So I call Stumpfig?

WILLIAM All right then—call him.
> (*The church carillon chimes*)

RONNIE They're at it in the apse again.

WILLIAM Nine o'clock. For heaven's sake, I was supposed to be in the office at a quarter to. (*Hurriedly puts on his coat, holds out his hand*) Ronnie, if I may coin a phrase, I'll never be able to thank you enough.

RONNIE Where are you going?

WILLIAM The office, of course. I'm terribly late.

RONNIE Nonsense. What difference does that make any more? What's old Lexy Potter but just another—you know what? Show your independence. Stick around while I call Stumpfig at least. (*As* RONNIE *crosses to the phone,* WILLIAM *hesitates and then, making the decision with an effort, remains while* RONNIE *lights an inevitable cigarette and dials, then speaks into the phone*) Six-O-three, please ... Hello, Paul. It's me. Did I wake you up? ... My God, I thought you always rose with dawn's first cowbell to gather edelweiss ... Never mind —Listen, you ought to be eternally grateful to me. I've found your man ... Yes, yes, everything you want, more than everything. He probably dotes on Swiss chocolate to boot ... I'm bringing him to lunch. Okay? ... Tote along all your illustrations and junk because he can take them right home and work on them tonight ... yes, Pavillon at one. But don't bring what's-her-name ... Leave her in bed ... But, Paul, listen, I'm going to the dentist so please not that table next to the Duchess of Windsor again. I will not curtsey after novocaine. (*He drops the receiver and turns to* WILLIAM) It's all fixed. He's delighted. (*Suddenly realizing*) My God, the dentist—nine-thirty! I daren't be an instant late. My dentist terrifies me. God knows what he does to me when I'm under sodium pentothal. (*Rushes toward the bathroom, yelling*) Jimmie, Jimmie, out. Out this instant. Scalp or no scalp—out!

(JIMMIE *emerges from the bathroom and* RONNIE *dashes into it*)

JIMMIE (*Hurrying toward* WILLIAM) William! Still here? Don't you realize the time? (*As he speaks, the phone rings*) There. You see? Lexy Potter. That bastard Lexy Potter. You've done it again.

(WILLIAM *goes to the phone and picks up the receiver*)

WILLIAM (*As he speaks, he is calm, strong, almost insultingly so*) Hello ... Oh, hello, Lexy ... Yes, I know. I'm a little late this morning, but I'll be there pretty soon. Yes, I realize about the reports ... All right, if you can't swing it without me, you'll just have to wait till I get there, won't you? ... So long, Lexy Potter.

(JIMMIE *has been listening, stunned by this show of independence. Then he gets it, and is wildly enthusiastic*)

63

JIMMIE (*Rushing to* WILLIAM *and grabbing his arms*) You've got it! Ronnie talked to you. He offered you the job.

WILLIAM Yes.

JIMMIE And it's definite?

WILLIAM Of course it's not definite. But they're going to give me a try.

JIMMIE Then it'll work, of course it will. Wow! Is it quite a good bit of money?

WILLIAM I didn't ask about the money.

JIMMIE Boy, no more bridge parties, no more fiddling, frittering. You working, me reading *The Possessed*. You will be working evenings, won't you? Every evening, I guess.

WILLIAM If it comes off, it'll be more than just evenings.

JIMMIE You don't mean . . . William, it's a real job, it's a real, full-time job?

WILLIAM Yes.

JIMMIE Then off, off. (*He grabs* WILLIAM's *arm and starts dragging him toward the door*) Grab a cab, dash to the office, thumb your nose at that little bastard Lexy Potter . . . No, no, don't thumb your nose, not yet, not till it's settled. But off, off, William. Shake a leg. (*He has got* WILLIAM *into the hall.* WILLIAM *"shakes a leg."* JIMMIE *picks up* WILLIAM's *coat, slings it over* WILLIAM's *shoulders like a cape and pushes him out of the door. He shuts the door, picks up the chain, is about to put it on and then drops it melodramatically*) What the hell? Let the marauders come. Let them all come.

(*He comes, wildly happy, into the living room*)   I did it. I did it. (*This strikes a chord. He beams*)   Tonight, old man, you did it. You did it. You did it. (*He starts singing* "I Could Have Danced All Night" *and begins waltzing riotously around the room. Suddenly he breaks off and runs to the bedroom door. He bangs on it vigorously*)   Hey ... hey ... Edith ... Wake up, Edith ... wake up ... slut.

EDITH (*Inside, groaning*)   What is it? For heaven's sake, what's the matter?

JIMMIE (*Banging again*)   Arise ... Arise, I say, oh, woman taken in adultery. Come out. Hear the news. Hear the wonderful news.

(*He starts humming* "The Rain in Spain" *and, grabbing the huntsmen shade off the lamp, begins a passionate tango*)

Curtain

Scene Two

Saturday morning, two weeks later, 11:30 A.M. There are two vases full of daffodils and tulips. WILLIAM *is sitting at the table, which is strewn with papers and large artist's illustrations for the first book. He is talking on the telephone, which stands on the table on a long extension cord. He is also working on the manuscript at the same time. He is excited, exuberant, a new man. A cup of coffee is on the desk.*

WILLIAM (*On phone*) As a matter of fact, I've finished the Third Section and I'd like to check with you on the order of the last two illustrations. It won't take five minutes . . . Okay.
(*He hangs up.* EDITH *enters from the bathroom in her blue robe*)

EDITH My, my, the last two weekends you're never off the phone. William, I turned that tub on half an hour ago and it's still only a quarter full. Can you imagine.

WILLIAM I was trying to get Stumpfig but he's not at the office yet.

EDITH Now don't start talking. You know you're not meant to talk. You're working. I'm just tippytoeing in and then sitting down quiet as a mouse waiting for the tub to fill.
(*She sits down*)

WILLIAM All this needs is a final toothcombing. (*Makes a correction*) I must cure myself of this guilty passion for semicolons.

66

EDITH (*Ruminative*) I think we can have Leon tonight with Basil. I just feel it in my bones. William!

WILLIAM Almost through.

EDITH After all, it was Leon's aunt in Blowing Rock who made that headcheese. Basil really should understand by now that people are sensitive when it's a question of family. And we can't go on forever like this with Basil making it so complicated. And I do want everyone at our celebration party.

WILLIAM It isn't a celebration. I don't even know if I have the job yet. Mr. Stumpfig may hate what I've done.

EDITH Well, I'll call Basil anyway and try to make him see.

WILLIAM (*Dropping pencil*) *Finito.*

EDITH (*Dialing on phone*) About time too. Every night last week without letting a soul come near you—and now Saturday morning even. It is odd the Lady from Philadelphia hasn't called. Having her weekend put off for the first time in nineteen years? I wouldn't have thought she'd take that lying down.

WILLIAM I explained about the rush work and the new job.

EDITH (*On phone, astonished*) Busy? Basil busy?
     (*She hangs up*)

WILLIAM Much as it may surprise you, Viola seemed to be pleased.

EDITH Of course she's pleased. We're all pleased.

WILLIAM (*Starts gathering up the manuscript and putting it in a Manila envelope*) I never thought I'd get it done so soon.

It's amazing how it all comes back. To begin with I thought I'd just have to hand in my resignation to Lexy Potter. But *this* work isn't work—it's Dexedrine. I'm going to be able to sail through the whole first text in my spare time.

EDITH (*Annoyed by this*) Are you really going out?

WILLIAM (*Selects some illustrations*) Right this minute. I'm crazy to find out how Bert reacts to an idea I've got for switching illustrations.
(*He starts for the hall and his coat*)

EDITH But you won't be late for lunch, will you? Please, William, not after I lied especially to Kenneth about my girl friend from Denver and having to show her the Guggenheim and *Camelot* and everything.

WILLIAM (*Crossing back to her with his coat*) Don't worry.

EDITH Are you crazy? Going out without your scarf?

WILLIAM Who needs a scarf?

EDITH My, you are excited about it all, aren't you?

WILLIAM Yes, I'm excited.
(WILLIAM *starts for the door*)

EDITH William.

WILLIAM Yes.

EDITH I don't pester you, do I? When I asked about the scarf, it wasn't pestering, was it? I feel so strange. Almost as if you'd gone away. And that's so silly, isn't it? I mean, nothing's changed. Just a different job and all. William, you're not going to let things change.

George Grizzard and Hume Cronyn as RONNIE JOHNSON and JIMMIE LUTON

WILLIAM (*Remembering her, coming back to kiss her*) Not till the *S.S. Pastores* sinks.

EDITH It was broken up for scrap years ago.

RONNIE (*Off*) William? Hey, William. (*Coming in, wearing a coat*) Why, my old pal the Sperm and You himself!

WILLIAM Hi, Ronnie.

RONNIE There I was at Grand Central and I couldn't resist dropping by to use your phone. Congratulations, maestro.

WILLIAM Congratulations on what?

RONNIE Hasn't Stumpfig called you?

WILLIAM Not yet.

RONNIE He will. He was drooling to me on the phone in Connecticut this morning at the dawn's earliest light. He's crazy about your first two sections. So's Blackwell. They're sicking their lawyers onto the contracts today.

WILLIAM You mean it?

RONNIE Didn't I tell you? Haven't you learned by now that I'm the most charming, colorful, talented, toothless prophet in North West Connecticut?

WILLIAM Look, I'm just dashing over to Blackwell for a minute. Stick around till I get back. Make Edith amuse you.

EDITH Yes, Ronnie, do stay.

WILLIAM (*At the door*) Oh, Edith, if Mr. Stumpfig calls, tell him I'll be with Bert and Mr. Mangan at Blackwell. See you.

EDITH All those names.

WILLIAM Hey, hey.
(*He exits*)

RONNIE (*Taking off his coat*) He seems very pulled together
at least.

EDITH You wouldn't believe it. You just wouldn't. Work,
work, work. And not being paid a cent yet. Not even know-
ing, so far as I can figure it, whether he's going to get the
job or not.

RONNIE He'll get it.

EDITH Ronnie, would you like a cup of inst?

RONNIE (*Delighted*) I'd adore a cup of inst. And—can I use
the phone?

EDITH If you can get to it before it starts ringing.

RONNIE (*Going to the phone, lighting a cigarette*) I've got a
free lunch date and I thought I'd get Basil off before I
weaken.
(*He dials*)

EDITH That will be nice for Basil. Basil's so fond of you.
Sometimes I can't understand. I mean, one man being so
fond of another man. But it's sweet.
(*She exits to the kitchenette*)

RONNIE (*On phone*) Basil? Hello, Basil, it's me. I just got in.
Look, some extraordinary miracle has taken place and I'm
free for lunch and I wondered . . . Well, great. Something's
gone right today, hasn't it? . . . What time? . . . Twelve-

thirty? . . . Yes, I can make it . . . Where? Oh yes, Long-champs, of course. The credit card.

(EDITH *comes out of the kitchen carrying two cups of coffee*)

EDITH Ronnie, let me talk to him when you're through.

RONNIE (*On phone*) Edith wants to talk to you . . . Edith, I said . . .

EDITH (*Puts down the coffee cups and takes the phone*) Basil, who were you talking to just now? Oh, Gristede's. It's about tonight—about the party. It's a terribly special occasion. William's got a wonderful new job and he wants to tell everyone about it. And after all it was Leon's aunt who made that headcheese and he does have a very deep feeling for his fam . . . But, Basil. (*She looks rather stunned*) No, Basil . . . Really, Basil. You mustn't. You . . .

RONNIE (*Taking phone*) Basil? It's me . . . Look, about the headcheese. Think of it this way. There hasn't been a head in Leon's family for generations so how can you expect their headcheese to be fresh? . . . No, Basil, it's not that funny . . . No, Basil . . . No, you can't repeat it . . . But poor old Leon, you wouldn't want to do him out of this lovely do, would you? . . . That's my boy . . . Give my love to Kitty, if she can hear the message over the steady ejection of fur balls.

(*He puts down the phone*)

EDITH (*Amazed*) It's all right?

RONNIE. Sure.

EDITH Drink your coffee while it's warm.

RONNIE (*Tasting it*)   Is this really inst? It tastes so good.

EDITH   Sure, it's inst. (*Sits down and toys with the daffodils*) Don't you like the daffodils? There's nothing so like spring as daffodils, is there?

RONNIE   From your garden?

EDITH   I'd say. And the tulips too. Aren't the tulips handsome?

RONNIE   You must have a bright green thumb.

EDITH   Oh, it isn't me so much. It's Kenneth, my husband. He's the gardener of the family.

RONNIE   So William has your husband to thank for the flowers?

EDITH   My, no. Kenneth didn't send them. Kenneth doesn't even know about William. He never has. Twenty years. Strange, isn't it? He's retired now, you know.

RONNIE   Has he?

EDITH   Or rather he's sort of semi-retired. Every now and then he goes off and consults, but . . . He can't do what he used to do. Do you think I ought to dress maybe?

RONNIE   I don't see why?

EDITH   I don't think I will. I feel like slopping around. Sometimes I feel like that, do you?

RONNIE   Slopping around's practically all I ever do.

EDITH   Kenneth doesn't like it. He's always been such a stickler. It's different with William. I can relax with William, can't you?

RONNIE I'd say.

EDITH Everyone can relax with William. Did I ever show you my picture of William on the beach at Cape May?

RONNIE I don't think you did.

EDITH I'll show it to you. (*Gets up and goes for her purse*) I always carry it around with me in my bag. I don't know why. Silly, isn't it? But Kenneth would never dream of looking in my bag—my private bag. (*She brings out a photograph and takes it to* RONNIE) Think of it. Over fifteen years ago on the beach at Cape May and I've still got him now.

RONNIE (*Taking the snapshot*) What is he doing?

EDITH Lighting a cigarette. It's a very characteristic pose of William, isn't it?

RONNIE Sort of stooping.

EDITH He's got such pretty feet. Have you ever noticed William's feet? It was Kenneth's feet that really did it. He's always been very good to me, but corns, bumps, bunions. I got so I could see them even when he had his shoes on.

RONNIE (*Giving back the snapshot*) Even in his gardening boots?

EDITH (*Putting the snapshot away in her bag*) Yes, I think so. And then he's always wanting to mess around. At his age.

RONNIE No.

EDITH Yes. Oh, my God. The tub. I forgot. (*Gets up and runs into the bathroom.* RONNIE *picks up a* Saturday Review *from the table, opens it to the crostic and takes out a pencil.* EDITH

73

comes back) It's almost full. But it's getting tepid. That's the trouble, you see. It's boiling hot when it comes out of the faucet—then it has to sit so long.

(*She sits down*)

RONNIE He hasn't done his doublecrostic this week. It's like the end of the world.

EDITH Oh, that's not all that's changed—I can tell you.

RONNIE Edith.

EDITH Yes, Ronnie.

RONNIE Would you miss William if he went away?

EDITH Of course I'd miss him. But he wouldn't go anywhere. Where would he go? Philadelphia? He'd never go back there. Ronnie, before William signs those contracts or whatever they are, do you really think the job's suitable for him?

RONNIE My God, he's twenty years younger already.

EDITH I think he's looking rather peaked. And then all that dashing around . . . celebrities . . . having lunch all over the place. It's so *different* for William. I found myself thinking just this morning. I wonder why Ronnie never took that job himself.

RONNIE Really, Edith. What are you being? The serpent in the garden?

EDITH A serpent? Me? What on earth do you mean? (*Rather embarrassed*) Oh, well, I guess I better get that tub. It's now or never. (*She starts to the bathroom.* WILLIAM *comes unexpectedly in at the front door, which* EDITH *has left off the chain.* EDITH *sees him*) My, back already? (*Goes and kisses him and points significantly at the bathroom*) The tub's full. I'll come out fresh as a daisy.

(WILLIAM *comes very quietly into the room*)

RONNIE Well, that was the quickest mission since the cosmonaut.

WILLIAM I didn't go. You got me so excited I called Stumpfig from a booth. Ronnie, you knew all along, didn't you?

RONNIE So he's told you. Oh, sure, sure, I knew.

WILLIAM Then for God's sake what was the idea of having everyone lie about it?

RONNIE Listen, Father William, if I help you, I help you in my own little special way. Stumpfig was crazy to get someone or his whole production schedule collapses. So I just suggested that, maybe if you get yourself all enthusiastic about the work first . . .

WILLIAM I'd be so beglamored that I'd be prepared to—to change my entire life? Pull up stakes? Start a whole new life in Europe?

RONNIE Why not? You dote on Europe. You never stop yodeling your old Geneva school song. And it's Geneva that's going to be your headquarters, isn't it?

WILLIAM (*Very quiet*) What's in this for you? Is Stumpfig paying you a commission?

RONNIE Well, well, in the long and checkered career of our friendship that's the first bitchy thing I've ever heard you say. That's progress—real progress. When he broke the news to you—what did you tell him?

WILLIAM Nothing. It came so quickly. He was just telling me about the contracts and— And then—he came out with it. Ronnie, goddam you, I'll never forgive you. This week was the most exciting week of my life. And now . . .

RONNIE Now—what?

WILLIAM You don't think I'm going to leave them all in the lurch, do you?

RONNIE Ah, ha—here we go.

WILLIAM But for God's sake, you know how they are. This place—why, it's the whole world to them.

RONNIE To *them?*

WILLIAM Think of Jimmie. Think of Basil—the way he behaves, there isn't a person in New York that'll let him through the door any more.

RONNIE Except William. The Big Fish, the dear old Mother Fish, swimming around with all her dear little barnacles, suckling them or whatever you do to barnacles.

WILLIAM You'd never see—

RONNIE See what? That you aren't really William Baker? That you're Jesus Christ, Esquire, dedicated to comforting the poor in spirit? Oh, come unto me all ye poor old drunks, ye pale sad neuters, ye suburban matrons with a wistful yen for adultery . . . Come unto my bosom and become barnacles.

WILLIAM Is that what *you* think *I* think of myself?

RONNIE Yes, and I've never heard such balls. It's the worst case of self-deception since the Wild Duck. Look, William, let's get this cruel-only-to-be-kind bit over with. Jimmie told me what happened at Merton.

WILLIAM (*Very shaken*) Jimmie told you!

RONNIE And don't make a thing about it because he only did it for your sake. Listen, William, time to look at our ugly faces in the mirror and have a lovely moment of truth. You've not been sheltering those poor little hangers-on of yours; you've been feeding off them—because for the last twenty years you've been holed up here scared pissy by a crazy little nymphet who knocked the pins out from under you way back in Merton in 1903. Edith fighting Jimmie, Basil fighting Leon—the Lady from Philadelphia fighting the whole field—just for the love of wonderful William. That's been your drug all these years. My God, why do I write novels about ladies doing odd things with Calabrian peasants? Why don't I grab my typewriter and just move in here?

WILLIAM Is Jimmie's analysis of my—my self-deception the same as yours?

RONNIE I haven't the faintest idea what poor Jimmie's analysis is. Probably it's a little more Krafft-Ebing, though.

WILLIAM But you think I've been needing them more than they need me?

RONNIE Now, William, don't go overboard. Fifty-fifty, I'd say. Just about fifty-fifty. But you don't have to worry about them. They'll survive. Barnacles always do.

WILLIAM And if I told you right now that I wouldn't dream of walking out on them and going to Europe . . . ?

RONNIE Well . . . Are you telling me?

77

WILLIAM   I said "if." If I told you that, would you say it was because I was scared of leaving my—my props behind?

JIMMIE (*Outside, trying to open the door*)   Damn, damn, goddam chain. Who's there? Who's put on that goddam chain? (RONNIE *gives* WILLIAM *a quizzical look.* WILLIAM *goes and lets* JIMMIE *in*)   So you've started putting the chain on when you're alone. Because you're so valuable these days, I suppose.

WILLIAM   Hi, Jimmie. What are all those groceries for?

JIMMIE   What do you think they're for? The animals at the zoo? (*Sees* RONNIE)   Oh, so *you're* here, Ronnie Johnson, Impresario of Geniuses. (*To* WILLIAM)   They're for your lunch. That's what they're for.

WILLIAM   But Edith's fixing lunch.

JIMMIE   *Edith's* here?

WILLIAM   Yes.

EDITH (*From the bathroom*)   Yoo-hoo.

JIMMIE   Ten days not seeing you, ten days not even being allowed to talk to you on the phone almost! And then Edith making lunch! William, are you losing your mind? When I called you on Thursday from White Plains, I distinctly said I was coming in early to fix your lunch. I repeated it twice. My God, you're so busy I suppose that a little thing like that would slip your mind, I suppose. My God, who do you think you are these days? Proust?

EDITH (*Coming out of the bathroom in her robe*)   Hi, Jimmie. Wonderful news. There's a party tonight. A special buffet bridge party.

78

JIMMIE Bridge!

EDITH And Leon's coming. Ronnie fixed it all with Basil. Basil and Leon are both coming.

JIMMIE (*To* WILLIAM) But—but it's Auden tonight. W. H. Auden at the Y.M.H.A. It's been fixed for six weeks. I've got the tickets. Okay, I give up. I just give up. Have a drink, Ronnie. I can't drink but at least someone's got to have a drink.
  (*He goes into the kitchenette*)

RONNIE Poor Jimmie.

EDITH He doesn't mind. He likes everything being dramatic. He's like a little child really. He's fond of me if he only knew it. (*Calling*) You are fond of me, aren't you, Jimmie?

JIMMIE (*Poking his head out of the kitchenette*) You've destroyed him. That's what you've done. (*Notices the daffodils*) More of Kenneth's daffodils, I see. One day I'm going to be an anonymous voice. (*Croaking*) "Your wife is doing it in the East Thirties." And he'll come dashing around here and he'll shoot the both of you in *flagrante delicto*. What a relief.
  (*He goes back into the kitchenette*)

RONNIE Well, William, aren't you going to tell them your news?

JIMMIE (*Popping out of the kitchenette*) What news?

EDITH Oh, just about signing contracts or something.

RONNIE I don't mean that. Go on, William. He who hesitates. (WILLIAM *does hesitate. Both* JIMMIE *and* EDITH *are watching him with growing concern*)

WILLIAM Well . . . well . . . it's . . . I've invited Mr. Stumpfig to the party tonight.

JIMMIE Stumpfig!

WILLIAM When we were talking on the phone about the con-
tract. He's a bridge enthusiast, apparently.

EDITH But Leon's coming. That's the whole point. Basil's going
to forgive Leon. How can Basil forgive Leon right there in
front of some terrible Swiss stranger?

RONNIE Poor Basil.

WILLIAM It won't kill him. You'll rather like old Stumpfig.
I've got very fond of him.

JIMMIE I suppose he's your best friend already . . . My God,
I'm going to have a cup of tea. If that's the nearest I can get
to dissipation, I'm just going to make myself a great big
pitch-black cup of tea.
  (*He goes into the kitchenette*)

EDITH (*Almost tearful*) There's no end to it. Absolutely no
end. I just wish I hadn't gone to all that trouble lying to
Kenneth. Or I wish my girl friend from Denver actually
had come. She's a lovely, warm, human, *real* individual.
  (*She flounces toward the bedroom*)

RONNIE Poor Edith. Okay, William, you've done your stalling.
Now tell them.
  (JIMMIE *and* EDITH *both turn and watch him*)

JIMMIE What is it? What's the matter?

WILLIAM (*Very quiet*) Ronnie, did you have to push it like
this?

RONNIE   Paul happens to be my friend too, you know. A friend that stands to lose thousands of dollars if his schedule gets loused up again. Oh, for God's sake, let's get this over with. This is my morning for sudden death. (*Turning to* JIMMIE *and* EDITH) William can have the job. It's a marvelous job. The contracts will be ready to sign in a week or two. But there's one aspect of it that he didn't know about till today. It means living permanently in Geneva.

JIMMIE   Geneva, Switzerland?

EDITH   But you can't, William. You can't possibly.

JIMMIE   Of course you can't.

RONNIE   (*Suddenly remembering*)   Oh, my God, Lili at the Swiss Pavillion. I'll have to cancel Basil.

  (*As the others rail at* WILLIAM, RONNIE *rushes over to the phone*)

EDITH   But what about the job you've got? What's wrong with it? It's always been a perfectly good job.

JIMMIE   (*Indicating the apartment*)   And what are you going to do with all this? Sublet? Break the lease?

EDITH   Yes, William, what about the lease?

JIMMIE   Sell everything? Throw it away? Discard all your mother's things? Why, that chair, it's an heirloom . . .

  (WILLIAM *stands in tense silence. He is really suffering*)

RONNIE   (*On phone*)   Hello, Basil, it's me. Listen, the saddest thing. I can't make lunch after all. I hate myself. I honestly do. But there's this Hollywood producer, Basil . . .

EDITH   (*Catching the word* BASIL)   And Basil. What about Basil?

JIMMIE (*Heavy sarcasm*)   Basil doesn't matter. Oh, no, forget all about Basil. Let Basil die.

RONNIE   Yes, Basil, of course. You know me. Next time we'll have a lovely, dazzling, interminable lunch at Longchamps.

EDITH   And Viola too, poor thing, poor pitiful thing, sitting there in Conshohocken with nothing, absolutely nothing to look forward to.

RONNIE (*Still on the phone, cupping the receiver, turning to* WILLIAM)   William, for God's sake, don't stand there, like St. Sebastian in full martyrdom. Put the poor bitches out of their suspense. Tell them how much you need them. Tell them you're far too itty-bitty a fish to swim away over the great big Atlantic and leave your little shoal behind.

EDITH (*Turning her fury on* RONNIE)   You calling us bitches when you started all this.

JIMMIE (*Turning on him*)   For God's sake, when I think of all the Philharmonic tickets I wasted on you.

RONNIE (*Still on phone*)   Oh, shut up. No, Basil. Not you. Good-bye, Basil. (*He puts down the phone and turns to* WILLIAM) Well, William?
   (*While all three watch* WILLIAM, *there is a long stony silence*)

WILLIAM   I'll be leaving for Europe on the *Queen Mary*. They're booking me a passage on the twenty-seventh of April, I believe.

The Curtain Falls

ACT THREE

Scene One

*The same—the same evening at 6:55 P.M. The table is set for
a buffet supper.* EDITH, *dressed for the party, comes out of the
bedroom.* JIMMIE, *in a suit, comes out of the kitchenette, carrying a sherry decanter and a glass. They are both very gloomy, but
the shock of what has happened has made them allies.*

JIMMIE (*Very sweet*) Edith, dear—can I get you anything?

EDITH No thank you, Jimmie dear. I do hope it's going to be
all right between Basil and Leon. I couldn't stand a scene—
not tonight of all nights.

JIMMIE Who the hell cares what happens tonight? I'm going
to have a glass of sherry.

EDITH Oh, Jimmie, should you?

JIMMIE For Chrissakes, only a tiny one.

EDITH But William says . . .

JIMMIE Williamwilliamwilliam. Do you always have to bow
down to William as if he was the Dalai Lama or something?
(*Studying the table*) I bet he doesn't take my Greek place
mats to Geneva. I bet he doesn't take a thing I've given him.

EDITH (*Looking at her watch*) He's been gone almost twenty
minutes. Twenty minutes just to go around the block to the
liquor store and buy a bottle of kirschwasser.

JIMMIE (*Lifting the glass, sniffing but not drinking*)   Kirschwasser—just because it's Swiss.

EDITH   Swiss. I suppose if someone entertained me in Switzerland they'd have to dash around the block and order a bottle of Napa Valley red wine.

JIMMIE   The buffet's all fixed, isn't it?

EDITH   Yes—and all the drink things are out in the kitchen.

JIMMIE   Then, for Chrissakes, let's sit for a bit. (*They both sit down together on the made-up daybed*) I feel terrible to my stomach.

EDITH   I just know he knew about Europe all along. Sneaky. And then sticking us with Mr. Stumpfig.

JIMMIE   William always does exactly what *he* wants to do.

EDITH   Well, that's men. They all do.

JIMMIE   You know what you said once when you got mad? About how you bet I got together with all my friends and laughed at you behind your back?

EDITH   Oh, Jimmie, for heaven's sake, we've forgotten all about that.

JIMMIE   But, Edith, I want you to understand. I get awful mad sometimes but I don't laugh.

EDITH   Men don't understand about women and romance and putting a man on a pedestal. They just think "the old bag" or something. He'll find someone in Geneva in a week, you'll

86

see. The first Frau or whatever they have that comes along and makes a fuss over him. It's all right for you. Every summer vacation from college you can go over. Maybe even go to Greece with him the way you always wanted.

JIMMIE   Every summer vacation? My God, do you know how long it took me to save for that Greece trip? Eight years. And then it was going student plane to Iceland and bicycles and hiking half the time with a goddam pack on my back. I hardly saw the shrine at Delphi, my feet were so sore with blisters.

EDITH   But what about me? If ever he comes back to the States for visits, it'll be times when Kenneth's at home. I know it will. That's just my luck. And as for going to Geneva—if you knew the times I have with Kenneth just getting from Tomsville to New York City. So there it is. Finished—after twenty years. And I never really had him to myself. The very first time we did it, he explained. I didn't really understand, but he explained—how it was sex and friendship and everything, but not real love, not the way love properly is. Twenty years of just sex and friendship. Like Viola, probably. Just like Viola.
   (*She breaks down*)

JIMMIE   Don't cry, for Chrissakes, Edith, it makes me nervous. (WILLIAM *enters carrying a wrapped liquor bottle. He is being very gay*)

WILLIAM   Hey, hey. (*Takes off his coat in the hall while* JIMMIE *and the recovered* EDITH *assume frigid masks. Then he comes into the room, stripping the paper off the bottle*) Look, kirschwasser. Eight dollars and twenty-nine cents.

JIMMIE   My God, spending all that money.

87

WILLIAM   It's the same brand we drank in Lausanne in '52.

JIMMIE   It choked me, I remember. Like drinking prussic acid.
   (*He flourishes his sherry glass to draw* WILLIAM's *attention to it*)

WILLIAM   Jimmie!

JIMMIE (*Belligerent*)   I want it.

WILLIAM   But you know how it is when you start!

JIMMIE   Who cares how it is when I start?

WILLIAM   This does happen to be my house, although it's getting increasingly hard to believe. Give it to me, Jimmie.

JIMMIE   You think I want to be sober? You think I want to stand there in cold blood and watch you kill Basil and Leon and everybody?

WILLIAM   Jimmie, I want you . . .

EDITH   I can't stand it. I can't stand a fight. Not tonight. I just can't.
   (*She snatches the glass from* JIMMIE)

JIMMIE (*He hadn't really planned to drink it; it was all show*)
   Edith . . . !

EDITH   Let him have his way. It's his house, isn't it? He's made that terribly plain.
   (*She exits into the kitchenette with the sherry*)

WILLIAM   Jimmie. Be nice. Please be nice just to help me get through the evening.

JIMMIE   I am nice.

WILLIAM   But it's what you wanted all along. Ever since we met you've been hammering away, yelling at me to get out of the rut. Without you and your help, I doubt whether I'd have got up the guts to break away. Jimmie, surely you know how grateful I am.

JIMMIE   (*Pleased in spite of himself*)   Oh, me. I just shoot my mouth off. All the time. With the girls at Wilma Morse too.

WILLIAM   It's much more than that. You've been a wonderful friend.

JIMMIE   You wouldn't ever read *The Possessed,* though. (*Pause*) William, would you? Would you maybe read it on the boat?
     (*The buzzer rings.* EDITH *hurries out of the kitchenette*)

EDITH   It isn't Basil. Basil always taps.
     (*She and* JIMMIE *stand together in uneasy alliance as* WILLIAM *opens the door and* PAUL STUMPFIG *enters. He is in his forties, dapper, rather handsome though a little bulbous and immensely sure of himself. He wears a coat with a fur collar and is carrying a package*)

WILLIAM   Well, good evening, Mr. Stumpfig.

STUMPFIG   Good evening, Mr. Baker. Am I late? You said for seven o'clock. It is four minutes past.

WILLIAM   You're not late at all. In fact you're the first guest.

STUMPFIG   (*Taking off his coat*)   Then I am early. Oh dear, it is the Swiss punctuality. It is bred in our bones like the racial prejudice in your Southerners. That great, great man William Faulkner. He is, no doubt, a friend of yours.

WILLIAM   No. I've never met him. Let me take your coat.
(*He takes it and drops it on a chair in the hall*)

STUMPFIG   Ah, no coat hangers, I see. Always when I go with Ronnie to his modish people, someone always comes running with a coat hanger.

WILLIAM   Do they? I'm terribly sorry. Would you like one?

STUMPFIG   Oh, no, no. I merely mark the difference in the different milieux. I am always marking differences, always studying. (*They come into the living room together.* STUMPFIG *is still carrying his package*) Why, this is charming. So simple. An American atelier. How do you say it? A garret.

WILLIAM   Yes, a garret. That's right. (*Introducing him to* EDITH) Mr. Stumpfig, I'd like you to meet Mrs. Maitland.

STUMPFIG   (*Kisses her somewhat reluctant hand*) How do you do?

EDITH   *Comment ça va?*

STUMPFIG   Ah, *français*. How charming. But I am a German Swiss.

WILLIAM   And this is my very good friend, Mr. Luton.

STUMPFIG   How do you do?

JIMMIE   Hello.

STUMPFIG   (*A little roguish*) Since Mr. Baker says I am the first guest, therefore you are not guests, therefore you live here. You are his *petits amis*. How charming. How open. How much I admire the American openness. If you knew what Calvin has done to us poor Swiss.

JIMMIE   At least he hasn't stopped you from speaking your mind.

STUMPFIG   You think so? Thank you. Thank you very much. (*Holding out his package to* EDITH) I brought this for Mr. Baker, but assuredly I shall present it to the Lady of the House.

EDITH (*Taking it*)   Why, thank you.

STUMPFIG   You will enjoy it extremely. It is Swiss chocolate. There is nothing more enjoyable than Swiss chocolate.

WILLIAM   What can we get you to drink? Some kirschwasser?

STUMPFIG   You have kirschwasser? How extraordinary. No, thank you. I will take some of your good bourbon and Seven-up.

JIMMIE (*Frigid*)   I'm afraid we don't have Seven-up in *this* house.

STUMPFIG   Then ginger ale—root beer—any of your national drinks.

JIMMIE   It'll have to be national soda water.
    (*He goes sulkily into the kitchenette*)

STUMPFIG (*To* EDITH)   I do not have to tell you, do I, madame, how brilliantly your lover has been working for us?

EDITH   Pardon me?

WILLIAM   He's paying me a compliment, Edith.

STUMPFIG Yes. I am. Without Mr. Baker, we would be truly in the soup—deep in the soup. But then we do not speak of business in society, do we? We shall speak of general conversation. You and your lover come with frequency to Switzerland?

EDITH I think you should understand something, Mr. Stumpfig. We're all plain-spoken people, I hope. Very plain-spoken, but . . .
(*She falters*)

STUMPFIG But—what, madame? It is all right. Quite all right I assure you. You will find no bigotry in me.

EDITH But . . . (*Defeated*) Well, skip it.

STUMPFIG (*To* WILLIAM) I was most surprised to hear you say you play bridge.

JIMMIE I don't. They do.

STUMPFIG I had always thought the American intellectual did not much play bridge. But I am glad to hear it because I . . . (*There is a tap on the door*) . . . am very fond of a good game of bridge.

EDITH That's Basil.

JIMMIE (*Starting for the door*) I'll get it.

WILLIAM No, Jimmie. I'll go.
(*He starts for the door*)

EDITH (*Intense hiss to* STUMPFIG) Mr. Stumpfig, this man who's coming—he doesn't know yet that William is going to Europe.

STUMPFIG   Ah ha, another *petit ami?*

JIMMIE   Good God.

EDITH   So please, please, don't say anything—not till William does. Do you understand?

STUMPFIG   I understand all things.
>   (WILLIAM *has opened the door,* BASIL *comes in. He is wearing the same rather odd hat and coat*)

BASIL   (*Puffing*)   Good evening, William dear. Is Leon here yet?

WILLIAM   Hello, Basil. No, not yet.

BASIL   I've got something to say to Leon. It's very, very funny. (*Quoting* RONNIE) Since there's been no heads in Leon's family for . . . (*Giggles*) No. I'm going to save it.

STUMPFIG   (*In the living room, to* JIMMIE *and* EDITH)   You are, of course, familiar with Madame de Staël.

EDITH   (*Rather vague*)   Oh, yes.

WILLIAM   Let me take your coat, Basil.

BASIL   (*Getting out of his coat*)   I understand from Edith that you're getting a new job. I hope you haven't done anything rash.

WILLIAM   Oh, no, it's terrifically exciting. I know you'll be delighted.

BASIL   (*Struggling with a sleeve*)   Oh, whew. Puff, puff.

STUMPFIG   (*To* JIMMIE *and* EDITH)   You will be most interested to hear that I have the great honor to live in the house of a cousin of Madame de Staël.

93

(JIMMIE *and* EDITH *murmur politely.* WILLIAM *takes* BASIL'S *coat.* BASIL *becomes conscious of* STUMPFIG)

BASIL   Who's that? There's someone sitting there.

WILLIAM (*Dropping the coat on a chair*)   That's my future employer. He's Swiss. A Swiss publisher.

BASIL (*Coming into the living room, ignoring the pitch of his voice*)   A Swiss publisher? Then I know him. I know all publishers *all* over the world.

JIMMIE   Hello, Basil.

BASIL   Good evening, Jimmie.

JIMMIE   A little vermouth?

BASIL   Oh, well, perhaps a sip. Those stairs. (JIMMIE *goes into the kitchenette*) Good evening, Edith dear.
   (*He kisses her*)

EDITH   Hello, Basil. How's the world been treating you?

BASIL   Kitty's pregnant.

EDITH   Oh, how cute.

BASIL   At least I think she's pregnant. (*Turns with great dignity to* STUMPFIG, *who has risen*) Good evening, sir.

WILLIAM   Basil, this is Mr. Stumpfig from Geneva. Mr. Stumpfig, this is my friend Basil Smythe. In his day he was a publisher too.

BASIL   Will you please repeat the name?

STUMPFIG (*Sitting down*)   Stumpfig. Paul Stumpfig.

94

BASIL Stumpfig. (*He ponders this for quite a long time*) You will soon meet an individual called Leon Purson. You must try to be forbearing with him and you mustn't on any account judge our country by the impression you get from him. I don't believe I know the name Stumpfig.

STUMPFIG Perhaps I came after your time, sir.

BASIL I doubt it. I keep up. I make a point of keeping up to date.

WILLIAM Won't you sit down, Basil?

BASIL Mr. Stumpfig is sitting in my chair.

STUMPFIG Oh, excuse me.
       (*He gets up*)

BASIL (*Sitting down*) I understand William has decided to take a job with you.

STUMPFIG That is correct.

BASIL You are very fortunate. When will he start work?

STUMPFIG It will be some time before it is all settled.

BASIL Then that's all right. I hope you have a good list. I had a very good list. Probably, at the time, the best list in Philadelphia. I published all—all but one—of the works of Rose Thaxter Turnbush.

STUMPFIG I do not hear of this lady, sir. She is perhaps one of your great Southern writers?

BASIL Certainly not. Rose Thaxter Turnbush always wrote for ladies and gentlemen.

JIMMIE (*Bringing* BASIL's *drink*) Here you are, Basil.

BASIL (*Taking it*) Ronnie was going to have lunch with me today but he didn't.

JIMMIE Why, that's too bad.

BASIL A movie producer, he said. I don't want to be acrimonious but I never really expected he'd come.
(*He sips his vermouth*)

EDITH (*Rather anxious*) Has your health been all right, Basil dear?

BASIL Oh, yes. I am very fit. A bit tired, though. It's the winter. It goes on so long. I mean, it's spring almost but the winter's been very long. (*Raises his glass to* WILLIAM) To your new job, William.

WILLIAM Thank you, Basil.

BASIL I only hope you'll be paid in dollars. I've never trusted the Swiss franc.

STUMPFIG (*Astounded*) But, sir, it's the soundest currency in the world.

BASIL I have never trusted the Swiss franc. You may sit down. I didn't mean you should stand just because you were sitting in my chair. You may talk to the others too because I have a proposition to make to William before a certain individual arrives. (*Grandly, to* EDITH) Will you forgive me, Edith, if I put my proposition to William?

EDITH Of course, Basil.

BASIL   It couldn't fit better with his change of job. It is all most auspicious. (*To* WILLIAM. *In spite of themselves, all the others stand or sit in silence, watching*) Now, William dear, you haven't been away all winter and neither have I and now it's off season in Florida and there's this bus. I've taken it before. It's a very good bus. It takes three days or is it four? And there's this little hotel in Miami. Not Miami Beach. Nobody wants to go there. But Miami itself. Well, I was thinking how you had two weeks coming from your old job but now it works just as well the other way. I have bought two round-trip tickets on the bus and I have wired the hotel—the Hotel Cecil—to reserve two rooms on the ocean side for April twenty-ninth. It's all to be at my expense. It's all to be a present from me.

> (JIMMIE *and* EDITH *converge, making a solid group of disapproval, watching* WILLIAM *icily*)

WILLIAM   Gosh, Basil, that's very sweet of you, but . . .

BASIL   It isn't sweet at all. You've always been very kind to me, which is more than can be said for some people. It'll give me great pleasure. We leave on Friday. I almost telephoned about it but I wanted it to be a surprise. Two surprises today. Your surprise and my surprise.

WILLIAM   But, Basil, this is terrible, but—but I don't think . . .

BASIL   Oh, yes, you can make it. Mr. Stumpfig is clearly an accommodating man, a very accommodating man. And I am paying for everything. You won't have to put your hand in your pocket.

WILLIAM   But, Basil, I should have explained. This new job, it's very exciting work, something I can really get my teeth

into at last and you've always known how drab and meaning-
less my other job was and . . .

BASIL I have bought the bus tickets. I have made the reservations.

WILLIAM I realize that, Basil, and I'd have loved to come. I
can't tell you how grateful I am for the thought. But by
April twenty-ninth I'll be gone.

BASIL Gone where?

WILLIAM Europe. Geneva. That'll be my headquarters. Geneva.
Basil, you'll come over and visit me, won't you? They've got
me an apartment. There'll be plenty of room. And you can
bring Kitty. Why not? There aren't any quarantine laws in
Switzerland.

BASIL When are you going, William?

WILLIAM In about ten days or less.

BASIL To Geneva?

WILLIAM That's right.

BASIL You'll like it, won't you? You always liked Geneva.

WILLIAM And the work, too. Just wait till you hear about it.

BASIL That's very good. I'm very happy for you. (*Gets up*)
Excuse me. It's my heartburn.
     (*He walks into the bathroom*)

EDITH (*In an outburst*) How could you, William? How could
you stand there and see his face? When it meant so much to
him. Reservations at the hotel and everything . . . reservations . . . the ocean side . . .

JIMMIE (*In an outburst*)   As if he could ever get to Switzerland. Basil? Basil with Pussikins in a little cat carrier?
   (*The front door opens and* RONNIE *comes in. He is carrying a wrapped liquor bottle. He hurries straight into the living room without taking off his coat.*)

RONNIE   Hi, everyone. Hello, hello, hello. Hello, Paul. Are you behaving yourself?

STUMPFIG   Yes. I behave myself very well indeed.

RONNIE (*Flourishing the bottle*)   I can't stay a minute. I just dropped by to leave a tiny contribution to the great event. A bottle of Beefeater. (*He looks around at the blank faces*) What's the matter? (*None of them speak. Very slowly* BASIL *comes out of the bathroom and walks stiffly toward them*) Hi, Basil. I feel terrible about lunch.

BASIL   That was all right. I went to Longchamps anyway. I felt like it. (*He goes to* WILLIAM) William, I want to say something. I want to say I'm very, very happy for you. You always deserved much more than you got in life. A great deal more. And I'm glad it has come your way. It would have been pleasant in Miami. I would have enjoyed it very much. I was quite looking forward to it. But I really shouldn't have left my research right at this moment. And now if you'll excuse me I think I'll go home. (*Turns to* STUMPFIG *with great dignity*) I'm sure you will excuse me, sir. To tell the truth, my cat has not been very well and there is a certain individual coming here whom I am not particularly anxious to meet. (*To the others*) Good-bye, all. No, William, I will let myself out. I don't want in any way to break up the conversation.
   (*While the others stand there, he goes up to the hall, gets*

into his coat and hat, and lets himself out the front door. All the others stand in silence. The door closes behind him. There is a pause. Then there is a crash. Instantly, WILLIAM, EDITH, JIMMIE *and* RONNIE *dash to the door.* WILLIAM *opens it. He,* JIMMIE *and* EDITH *dash out.* RONNIE *stands at the door, looking down. Offstage we hear muffled voices, and then* EDITH *screams, "You see, William? You see what you've done?"* RONNIE *turns slowly from the door to* STUMPFIG)

STUMPFIG   Is it serious?

RONNIE   My God, I believe he's dead—the poor old son-of-a-bitch.

Curtain

Scene Two

The same—one week later. The apartment is partially dismantled. The sconces above the table have disappeared. There are two almost-packed cartons on the bed. A small overnight bag, belonging to JIMMIE, *is somewhere on the floor. There are also old newspapers around, for packing.* BASIL'S *cat is sitting on* JIMMIE's *jacket, which is thrown on* BASIL'S *chair.*

JIMMIE, in shirt sleeves, comes out of the kitchen carrying the sherry decanter and a glass. He takes a gulp of sherry. He crosses to his overnight bag. As he does so, he notices the cat.

JIMMIE You. In here again. Getting hairs over everything. Don't look so pleased with yourself. (*He picks it up*) William's going to get all your money. You're a pauper. (*Throws it in the bathroom and shuts the door. Still holding his sherry glass he crosses toward his bag, notices a measuring cup on the table, and picks it up*) My measuring cup. (*He takes it to his overnight bag and starts packing it in newspaper*)

WILLIAM (*Calling from the bedroom*) Jimmie. (JIMMIE *ignores him but hides his sherry glass in a scrap basket*) Jimmie!

JIMMIE (*Calling, very dignified and icy*) I heard you the first time. I can't be everywhere at once.

WILLIAM (*Appearing from the bedroom, wearing a beige cardigan and carrying a pair of slippers*) Are these your slippers?

101

JIMMIE You know they are. But you don't think I came all the way from White Plains just to pick up a pair of slippers, do you? (*Snatches the slippers and puts them in the bag*) There's that beige sweater you borrowed too. (*Indicates it*) I'd like it, please. (WILLIAM *meekly takes off the sweater*) I bet you've stretched it out of all recognition. (*Folds it*) That cat of yours was in here again, crawling over everything. I dumped it in the bathroom. God knows what'll happen when she boards the *Queen Mary*. Mutiny probably. (WILLIAM *returns to the bedroom.* JIMMIE *goes into the kitchenette.* JIMMIE *returns, carrying the Greek place mats, simultaneously with* WILLIAM, *who is bringing some photographs to pack in the carton*) William, I don't suppose you're going to take these Greek place mats with you to Geneva, are you?

WILLIAM (*Embarrassed*) Well, well, I . . .

JIMMIE Because if you're not, I'm sure George and Muriel would appreciate them. They adore everything Greek.

WILLIAM Who are George and Muriel?

JIMMIE Oh, just friends. They spent a whole winter on Hydra. They're artists. I met them at the Met. *La Gioconda*.

WILLIAM Then, okay, okay. If George and Muriel want the mats—okay.

JIMMIE Thank you.
    (*He takes the mats and starts putting them in his bag. There is a long, pregnant pause*)

WILLIAM Jimmie.

JIMMIE Yes, William.

WILLIAM   I am going to see you again, aren't I?

JIMMIE   Of course. I'll make a point of coming to Edith's terrible going-away party on the boat. Probably I'll bring a
huge basket of fruit.

WILLIAM   I mean, I am going to see you again before I go.

JIMMIE   I seem to be awfully busy these days.

WILLIAM   George and Muriel?

JIMMIE   Yes, them—and Horace.

WILLIAM   You're certainly collecting a whole raft of new
friends, aren't you?

JIMMIE   What did you expect me to do? Die in an ambulance
like Basil and probably wind up on a table being dissected
by medical students? Well, that's everything. If I dash, I
can just make the twelve thirty-seven.

WILLIAM   Jimmie.

JIMMIE   What is it now?

WILLIAM   I just thought that maybe you'd let me take you out
to lunch.

JIMMIE   Oh, so no one's invited you to Pavillon today. I suppose you just happened to have a free lunch date so you
might as well get me off the way Ronnie used to get Basil off.

WILLIAM   Jimmie, please don't do this.

JIMMIE   Do—what?

WILLIAM   You know how I feel about Basil.

103

JIMMIE   Do I? Do I know anything you feel these days?

WILLIAM   You think I'll ever forget Miami and the Hotel Cecil?

JIMMIE   Oh, sure, you'll remember. Every now and then. Someday in Rome or Paris when you're giving dinner to some celebrity—on Basil's money, of course—you'll think: My, my, how poor old Basil loved me. And a tear will drop into your crêpes suzettes. Too bad Edith and I and Leon couldn't have obliged with little heart attacks too. Or maybe you'd like us all to commit mass hari-kari on the sun deck of the *Queen Mary*.

WILLIAM   My God, you're the blackmailer of all time, aren't you?

JIMMIE   (*Furious, whipping off his glasses as if ready for a fist fight*) Me? A blackmailer? Me? How dare you say that to me.

WILLIAM   What do you expect me to do? Punish myself again because Basil's dead? Spend another twenty years in penance? Did it help that girl in Merton that I tried, convicted, and sentenced myself to twenty years in Lexy Potter's penitentiary? My God, I want this job. I want it more than I wanted to be president of Merton. And I need it now much, much more because it's my last chance. (*His voice changes to a note of pleading*) You don't think I want to leave you all, do you? But haven't you looked at me once in the past few weeks? Haven't you been able to see the difference between a zombie—and a man who's alive?

JIMMIE   So, all this time you've been punishing yourself for some goddam imaginary sin. Suffering all day at the office and then coming back here to put up with Edith and me. For twenty years I've been receiving individualized, person-to-person therapy from a saint—and absolutely free of charge, too.

(*He makes a lunge for the front door.* WILLIAM *catches him by the arm and makes him sit in* BASIL's *chair*)

WILLIAM (*Looking down at him*) You told Ronnie about Merton, didn't you?

JIMMIE Christ. All right. Yes, I did.

WILLIAM A sad, sad story, wasn't it? Me and my imaginary sin. Poor, innocent William, destroyed by the neurotic daughter of the most influential trustee. (*He brings this out of himself with an immense effort*) I slept with her. Of course I slept with her just because she *was* a trustee's daughter. That's how much I wanted that job. And I can't tell you how easy it was. She was plain; she was naïve, she was lonely. A couple of rolls in the hay and we were Romeo and Juliet. We were all set to run off and get married. And then—when it came to the point—I panicked. I sent her a telegram with the one word: Sorry. Then I went out and got drunk. When I came home and found her, I called Viola. There was no one else I could think of. You see, I didn't know you in those days, Jimmie. So much for kind, wonderful William playing St. Francis to the downtrodden.

JIMMIE (*He sits for a long time very quietly*) I'm sorry I said that. (*He gets up*) William, have you told that story to anyone else? The true story, I mean?

WILLIAM No.

JIMMIE Not even to Edith or the Lady from Philadelphia?

WILLIAM God, no.

JIMMIE I'm the only one?

WILLIAM The only one.

JIMMIE I—William, I . . . There's something I want to tell you, too. I . . . I . . .
(*Overcome with emotion, he runs over and takes his concealed sherry glass out of the scrap basket*)

WILLIAM (*Smiling*) Is that what you want to tell me? That you've snitched a glass of my sherry?

JIMMIE Oh, no, that's just because I've been so nervous. It's nothing. Just like a Miltown or something. William, I know you know how fond of you I've been. And I am. Of course I am. But it isn't just that. It's more. William, we've never talked about this and I never thought I would, but . . . but . . .

WILLIAM Jimmie, do you think I didn't know?

JIMMIE (*Rather annoyed*) Know what? (WILLIAM *puts his hand lightly on* JIMMIE's *arm*) You knew and you didn't mind?

WILLIAM Who am I to mind? People are the way they are. And that's how it ought to be. (*They stand looking at each other. Then* WILLIAM *breaks it for them both*) We'l, I better finish packing those cartons. The Railway Express is supposed to show up at one-thirty.
(WILLIAM *goes into the bedroom.* JIMMIE *is left alone for the moment, which is probably the happiest in his life.* WILLIAM *comes out of the bedroom, carrying a pile of uniform leather-bound books, and starts to carry them over to the cartons*)

106

JIMMIE William, that's *The Possessed!* The whole Dostoevski set I gave you.

WILLIAM Sure.
(*He starts putting them in the carton*)

JIMMIE You're taking them with you to Europe?

WILLIAM I've got to have something to get me through those cold Swiss evenings, don't I?

JIMMIE (*Stands, totally defeated by joy, then he starts for the door*) William, I—I'm out of cigarettes. I think I'll just run around the block. I think . . . I . . . No, I won't take the bag. I'll be back. God knows, there's dozens of things that *someone* has to do around here.
(JIMMIE *exits. Alone,* WILLIAM *picks up* The Possessed *and dips into it.* STUMPFIG *appears on the landing and rings.* WILLIAM *lets him in*)

WILLIAM Mr. Stumpfig. What a pleasant surprise.

STUMPFIG Good morning, Mr. Baker. Ronnie is not here yet?

WILLIAM Why, no. Is he coming?

STUMPFIG He arranged for me to meet him here at twelve-thirty on my way to lunch. It is now twelve thirty-two.

WILLIAM Then he's bound to be here at twelve thirty-seven. Sit down, sit down. Let me get you a hanger for your coat.

STUMPFIG No, thank you. I keep my coat.

WILLIAM Then a glass of sherry maybe?

STUMPFIG You still perhaps have your kirschwasser?

WILLIAM Of course.

STUMPFIG I think I take kirschwasser.

WILLIAM All right.
  (*He goes into the kitchenette*)

STUMPFIG (*Producing a package*) I have brought you some
more Swiss chocolate. It is a different brand. But it is just as
enjoyable.

WILLIAM (*Coming out of the kitchenette with a glass*) Thanks.
  (*He takes the package*)

STUMPFIG I thought to myself. I am sure that Mr. Baker's
charming mistress took the chocolate for herself. I am sure
Mr. Baker has none.

WILLIAM As a matter of fact, you were quite right. Look, Mr.
Stumpfig, I'm glad you're here because I've just been going
through that final section again. I'm still not completely
satisfied with the last paragraph. (*Draws the reluctant* STUMP-
FIG *over to the table*) You see? It's just a question of bringing
this in a little earlier, and that way, you'll find, the whole
thing is modified by . . .
  (*The door opens and* RONNIE *comes hurrying in with
his coat on*)

RONNIE Hello, William.

WILLIAM Hi, Ronnie.

RONNIE I'm sorry, Paul. I just couldn't get away from that
spooky dentist. He's been drilling me for hours. I'm in agony.
Have you told him?

STUMPFIG   I have said nothing. I wait for you. Without you I do not have the courage.

WILLIAM   (*Realizing*)   You don't want me.

RONNIE   William, it isn't that exactly. Paul thinks what you did was fine.

STUMPFIG   Yes, Mr. Baker. Speaking for me, I say you did an excellent job. But Mr. Mangan decided to check with a qualified biologist to make sure that in changing the original text you had not altered the scientific facts. I'm afraid the biologist found quite many errors. Not large ones, of course, but in a work of this magnitude . . .

WILLIAM   But, for God's sake, that's only natural. I'm not meant to be an up-to-date biologist. Nobody ever said I was. Have them correct the errors and I'll see it gets back into good English.

RONNIE   Paul, that's only a miserable little alibi and you know it. Tell him the real reason.

STUMPFIG   I—I do not know how to say it. Truly, I find it most painful.

RONNIE   (*Sarcastic*)   How my heart bleeds for you. (*To* WILLIAM)   Bill Clangdon's free after all.

STUMPFIG   Mr. Clangdon has been able to get out of his prior commitment. And under the circumstances . . . Mr. Baker, I do feel as things have turned out we are treating you badly. But it is not as if the contracts were signed . . . (*Feels in his pocket*)   I have talked it over with Mr. Mangan and we thought . . . (*Produces the envelope*)   Does five hundred dollars seem too little to compensate you for what you have done?

WILLIAM (*Takes the envelope*) No, I don't think that's too little.

STUMPFIG You do understand, Mr. Baker. Mr. Clangdon is an international name. Names mean everything today.

RONNIE For God's sake, Paul, that's enough. Get the hell off to Pavillon and gorge yourself.

STUMPFIG (*Holding out his hand to* WILLIAM) Mr. Baker.

WILLIAM (*Taking his hand*) It was fun. I enjoyed it a lot. (*Turning to the manuscript on the table*) Don't you want to take all this stuff?

STUMPFIG No, no. Do not trouble. I shall send a messenger for them. I . . .

RONNIE Paul, get out.

STUMPFIG But I'll be seeing you.

RONNIE Sure, around.

STUMPFIG But it's tonight at the Clangdons', isn't it? They told me you'd promised to be there.

RONNIE Get your ass over to Pavillon. (STUMPFIG *goes out and closes the door behind him.* RONNIE *watches* WILLIAM) The bastards. If you'd heard how they groveled to that goddam Clangdon, offering him the moon.

WILLIAM (*Very quiet*) I can imagine.

RONNIE William, I'm sorry. It seemed such a brilliant idea. I never dreamed it could go wrong.

WILLIAM   One of the things about ideas is that they're always going wrong. (*He picks up the fish toy which has been standing on the table by the manuscripts*)   Well, it seems I was destined for a little pond after all. Not a very big pond fish, either. Just one of the small ones swimming around with a tiny delusion of grandeur. Thanks anyway, Ronnie. It was quite an experience for a little minnow to skim through the air for a while like a glamorous flying fish. If you'll pardon a rather confused and fishy simile.

RONNIE   You're taking this very well, William.

WILLIAM (*Putting the toy down*)   Maybe you were right about me that very first day. Maybe I'm relieved it's all over. Maybe I'd have missed those bridge evenings just as much as Basil.

RONNIE   You know you don't believe that.

WILLIAM   I might as well believe it, don't you think? From now on.
     (*The front door opens and* JIMMIE *and* EDITH *come in.* JIMMIE *is smiling happily.* EDITH, *rather shy, is carrying a large wrapped package*)

JIMMIE   He left the chain off. Wouldn't you know?
     (*He puts the chain back in place*)

RONNIE   William, I can't face this. (*Hurries toward the bathroom*)   Hi, Jimmie. Hi, Edith.

JIMMIE and EDITH   Hi, Ronnie.

RONNIE (*Clapping a hand to his cheek*)   My tooth. The dentist insists I gargle every ten seconds with scalding hot toilet tissue.
     (*He disappears into the bathroom*)

EDITH (*Coming toward* WILLIAM) Jimmie and I met on the stairs. Look, a peace offering from me. Just to say how sorry I am for being so naggy and selfish and mean all week.

JIMMIE What is it for Chrissakes—another lampshade?

EDITH (*Tearing off the wrapping and revealing a large red tartan animal carrier*) It's for Pussikins on the *Queen Mary*. See how grand it is.

WILLIAM Why, thank you, Edith, but you shouldn't have spent all that money.

JIMMIE Brother, if she spits up a fur ball in that—throw her overboard, William.

EDITH It came in a blue tartan too, but I thought the red had much more style.

WILLIAM I'm sure the red is much better-looking.

JIMMIE (*Sensing the difference in* WILLIAM) What's the matter, William?

EDITH Why, is something the matter?

WILLIAM They've got the man they always wanted—Bill Clangdon.

EDITH You mean it's off?

WILLIAM It's off.

JIMMIE But they can't do that to you.

WILLIAM They always wanted him. They got him.

JIMMIE And all that work—all gone for nothing?

WILLIAM They gave me five hundred dollars and some more Swiss chocolate.

EDITH So you'll be staying after all. Jimmie, he's staying. We must have a party.

WILLIAM (*Picking up the cat carrier and examining it*) This certainly is a very handsome cat carrier.
(*The phone rings.* RONNIE *comes running out of the bathroom*)

RONNIE Sorry, all. That'll be for me. I left the number. (*He picks up the phone*) Hello? . . . Yes, it's me . . . Hi, Dorothea . . . Naomi? Now keep your shirt on. Of course I'm not at Naomi's. It's just that place I always stay, the one near Grand Central . . . Look, honey, I'm glad you called because I'm going to be late for our terrible cup of tea at the Plaza. I've got to see a lawyer after lunch . . . Yeah, I just heard this morning. Some poor old friend of mine died last week, left me his entire estate . . . No, sweetie, not now . . . not now, I say . . . See you. Love, love, love.
(RONNIE *hangs up.* WILLIAM *has been listening in enigmatic silence, but both* EDITH *and* JIMMIE *are glaring at* RONNIE *as if he were Satan*)

JIMMIE Basil left his entire estate to you?

RONNIE Including Pussikins. God knows what I'll do with her. Loan her to the Smithsonian?

WILLIAM I'll keep the cat.

RONNIE Why, William, that's angelic of you.

EDITH But William was to have had that money. William. Basil always promised it to William.

RONNIE   I'm sorry, William. I didn't have any idea. But you know how he was always changing that will. It just happened to be my week, I guess.

JIMMIE   Now we know what sort of a friend you are.

RONNIE   Would you also like to know how much the entire estate of Basil Edgar Cunningham Smythe deceased amounts to? Three thousand, two hundred and seven dollars and nineteen cents—and two bus tickets to Florida. The poor old bastard had been living on his capital for years. (*He turns to* WILLIAM) Gosh, William, I couldn't be more stunned about everything. It's all monstrous. But one of these days I'll come up with an absolutely dazzling new proposition. I swear it. (*He looks at his watch*) Oh, God, I've got to dash. The Four Seasons at one. A dear old friend just flew in from London. A playwright. One of those angry young men.

WILLIAM (*With muted irony*)   What do young men have to be angry about?
   (*The phone rings.* RONNIE *jumps to answer it*)

RONNIE (*On phone*)   Hello, it's me . . . Who? . . . Oh, wait a minute. (*Cups the receiver, holds it toward* WILLIAM, *rather surprised that there can be a call which isn't for him*) It's for you, William. I think it's the Lady from Philadelphia. Shall I . . .?

WILLIAM   No. I'll talk to her.

RONNIE (*Handing him the phone*)   Well, see you, William. (*Pats his arm*) Love, love, love.
   (*He starts for the front door*)

WILLIAM (*On phone*)   Hey, hey, Viola . . . Yes, I'm fine . . . He is? That's good news. I guess the salve from the vet was

the right thing after all . . . Yes, of course I'm coming . . .
this Friday . . . the usual time . . . Look, Viola, I'm glad the
dog's all right because I've inherited a cat and I can't leave
it alone here. I'll have to bring it with me . . . Yes, it's a very
well-behaved cat. An occasional fur ball is all.

    (RONNIE, *who has reached the door, opens it. It sticks on
the chain*)

RONNIE Goddam chain.

    (*He releases the chain and exits*)

WILLIAM (*On phone*) Of course I can bring it on the train . . .
in a cat carrier. A very handsome cat carrier. Red tartan . . .
No, I didn't buy it. Someone gave it to me . . . Oh, no one
you know. Just a friend . . . Sure I'm fond of her—him. I'm
fond of all my friends. There's not much point to life, is
there, if you're not fond of your friends?

    (*The chimes sound from the church as*

The Curtain Falls